THE UNBELIEVABLES

The Remarkable Rise of Leicester City

THE 2015/16 PREMIER LEAGUE CHAMPIONS

THE UNBELIEVABLES

The Remarkable Rise of Leicester City

THE 2015/16 PREMIER LEAGUE CHAMPIONS

David Bevan

First published by deCoubertin Books Ltd in 2016.

deCoubertin Books, Basecamp, Studio N, Baltic Creative Campus,
Jamaica Street, Liverpool, L1 0AH

www.decoubertin.co.uk

ISBN 978-1-909245-44-0

A CIP catalogue record for this book is available from the British Library.

Cover design by Dave Williams

Layout by Milkyone Creative

This book is dedicated to the memory of:

Tom Bedford
Paul 'Larry' Flanagan
Samuel Garner
Ian Midgley
Jasbir Rupra
Tony Skeffington

FOREWORD

Alan Birchenall MBE

WHEN I PLAYED FOR LEICESTER CITY IN THE 1970S, I'D MEET THE rest of the players in the café on the corner of Filbert Street before training for an egg and bacon butty. We'd have to change at the stadium and then head up to the training ground at Belvoir Drive a couple of miles away. Sometimes we'd jog there. These days they do a warm-up session but we'd already done it in those days. By the time we got to Belvoir Drive, we were knackered.

There were two reasons I chose Leicester: they played good football and the atmosphere at Filbert Street was brilliant.

Four decades on, the atmosphere at the King Power has played a part in the greatest achievement in Leicester City's history.

The club brought in cardboard clappers for every fan during the great escape from relegation in 2015. All the reservations people had went out the window and everyone got involved in making noise to support the team. The feeling built. The results started to build too and the great escape in itself was a story. We carried that on into this season. They say new stadiums don't create atmosphere. Visiting managers and coaches all tell me the King Power has the best atmosphere in football.

I stand in the centre circle as the players run out to the Post Horn Gallop before games and the noise from the fans always makes the hairs on the back of my neck stand on end. Wes Morgan tells me it's brilliant and gives the players a lift.

As the games went on, people said the bubble would burst. That provided a challenge the lads took and turned into a positive. They were determined to prove how good they were.

We didn't need possession to win. Everybody tries to copy Barcelona but they've got Lionel Messi up front. We played to our strengths and eventually the critics had to admit we were a good team. A great team. A team that's made history.

I've enjoyed it all, standing in the tunnel and watching as we took whatever was thrown at us and came back from it every time.

In May, I got the chance to walk out of that tunnel holding the Premier League trophy.

I'd been sat at home at ten o'clock on the Wednesday night beforehand. The chief executive, Susan Whelan, rang me and I thought I was in for a rollicking. I asked what I'd done. She laughed and said 'no, we've had a meeting and the club would like you to walk out with the trophy'. I couldn't believe it.

We were lined up in the tunnel after the final whistle and I asked to hold the trophy. The guy looking after it asked if I was ready. It turns out I wasn't. I stood there for five minutes and it was getting heavy! You only ever see big guys lift the trophy. By the time I walked out onto the pitch, it almost felt like I'd been playing.

As part of my role as club ambassador, I hold a remembrance service in the memorial garden at the King Power every summer.

After family, your football club is the most important thing in your life. It'll mean so much to the families of City fans who have passed away, who didn't live to see the greatest achievement in our club's history, that we will be able to stand there and say we are the champions of England.

Leicester City: champions of England.

Alan Birchenall, May 2016

THE MOMENT EVERYTHING CHANGED

Sunday 23 October 2011

DAVID SILVA, MANCHESTER CITY'S MIDFIELD MAGICIAN, REACHES out and controls the ball at an awkward height. It sits up nicely to be played on the volley. Silva cushions a pass over the halfway line into the path of team-mate Edin Džeko.

Rio Ferdinand and Chris Smalling, Manchester United old and new, give chase. They can't get there.

Džeko takes two touches to set himself and passes the ball into the corner of the net at David De Gea's near post.

The Old Trafford scoreboard reads: Manchester United 1 Manchester City 6.

And we celebrate. We actually celebrate. Across the country, across the world, we celebrate.

This day will change the course of Premier League history.

Manchester United fans call us ABUs – Anyone But United. We can't argue. It's true. Isn't it time for a change?

A title race ensues between the two Manchester clubs. The battle goes deep into stoppage time in the final game of the season before Sergio Agüero scores the goal that makes Manchester City the champions of England, only the fifth club to lift the trophy since the Premier League began in 1992. We wonder how long it will be until a sixth is added to the list.

In the meantime, we're happy. Even if Manchester City owner Sheikh Mansour has spent hundreds of millions of pounds in an attempt to topple Sir Alex Ferguson's United, at least it's something different.

The only problem is that it's also completely meaningless to the club we love. These events are taking place in Manchester – at Old Trafford and the Etihad Stadium - but they feel a million miles away. They only exist to us on television. It's another world. Because we are Leicester City and the Premier League is a distant dream.

The day after that tumultuous Manchester derby, Sven-Göran Eriksson is sacked as manager of Leicester City having won only five of the first thirteen Championship games of the season.

Eriksson's removal signals a change of direction for the club's Thai owners. They will eventually turn to a manager who left Leicester a year earlier: Nigel Pearson - a man who will clear out the deadwood, assemble an exceptional scouting team, encourage investment in the medical and sports science departments and restore a winning mentality.

Saturday 6 February 2016
THE MANCHESTER CITY GOALKEEPER JOE HART IS STANDING IN the same six-yard box he left in celebration when that unforgettable Agüero goal hit the net at the opposite end of the Etihad Stadium four years earlier.

Now he can only fall slowly backward as the ball flies past him.

And we celebrate. We really celebrate. Across the country, across the world, others celebrate.

This goal will change the course of Premier League history.

THE NEARLY MEN: 1884 – 2000

WE ARE LEICESTER CITY FOOTBALL CLUB. WE WERE FORMED sixteen years before the end of the nineteenth century. Through those years and the hundred that followed and the sixteen years into the twenty-first century, we never won the league. We came close in 1929 and again in 1963 but we never quite managed it.

It seems that every club and their fans have enjoyed time in the limelight.

Newcastle United haven't won the league or cup for over fifty years but they have ten altogether gathering dust in their trophy cabinet. Southampton, who have never won the English top flight, have their 1976 FA Cup success to look back upon with pride. West Ham United have never won the league either but have three FA Cups to their name.

If you take major honours out of the equation and consider the other measures of the size of a football club – the stadium, the fanbase, its most famous players and managers, its potential and reputation – Leicester City are arguably the biggest never to have won the league or FA Cup, followed by Stoke City, Birmingham City, Norwich City and Middlesbrough.

In football, it is often said that the fans are the club; that chairmen, board members, managers, players and backroom staff all come and go and the fans remain, forming the true continuity in a club's history. We hear this whenever a club finds itself in crisis or, in the case of most big Premier League clubs, they've lost two games in a row. It usually means that the fans want heads to roll.

Nobody says the fans are the club when the club is doing well.

All that's different, of course, is that the team is winning instead of losing. They're scoring more goals than the opposition and they're doing it week after week after week. If those weeks turn into months and months turn into years, the structure of English football makes it possible for something amazing to happen.

It's possible, but only just. Everything has to come together at once and that's rare.

Filbert Street in the 1960s: one of the most lop-sided grounds in the country, with two large stands to the south and west and two glorified sheds to the north and east; rows of bicycles chained to the railings on match days and players arriving alongside supporters. You can define it now by what didn't exist: no segregation of fans; no substitutes; no names on shirts and certainly no diving.

The swinging sixties were arguably Leicester City's golden era, during which we reached the FA Cup Final on three occasions. Like our first appearance in 1949, however, we lost at Wembley each time: 1961, 1963, 1969. When looking back through history, it seems that City would be tagged as the nearly men of English football if anyone cared enough for such a tag to exist.

Take our three main rivals: Nottingham Forest, Derby County and Coventry City.

Four years have passed since Leicester and Coventry last contested the M69 derby, named after the motorway that connects two cities similar in population. Their football clubs could and should be similar too, but Coventry have won just one of the past sixteen games between the sides and haven't finished in the top six of any division since 1970 – seven years before the construction of the M69 was completed.

The 1970s were the glory years for football in the East Midlands but, while Derby County won the league twice and Nottingham Forest ended the decade as kings of Europe, Leicester City played the role of the great entertainers. Jimmy Bloomfield constructed a team full of attacking talent – Frank Worthington, Keith Weller, Lenny Glover – who were heroes at Filbert Street but couldn't convert that quality into silverware.

When Bloomfield left, things got worse. 1978 was a particular low point, as newly-promoted Forest won the league title under Brian Clough and we finished bottom of the table.

If the 1970s were an era of great entertainment, the 1980s brought even greater highs and lows. The first part of the decade was spent yo-yoing between the First and Second Divisions despite the emergence of one of England's greatest strikers, Gary Lineker.

This is another hallmark of Leicester City's history. Some of the most celebrated English footballers of all time have played for the club early in their careers – Gordon Banks and Peter Shilton being the two other obvious examples – without quite managing to contribute to collective success at club level.

In the late 1980s, things took a turn for the worse. City weren't yo-yoing any more. We were mid-table in the Second Division and it seemed the only place we were headed next was down. This was an era of low crowds, low entertainment value and a low-flying aeroplane hauling a banner demanding the departure of manager David Pleat and chairman Terry Shipman.

On 11 May 1991, after both men had gone, City faced Oxford United at Filbert Street needing to better West Bromwich Albion's result against Bristol Rovers in Bath. If we didn't, we would be relegated to the third tier of English football for the first time.

In the lead-up to the game, the Leicester Mercury published a map of Third Division grounds for City supporters to cut out and keep. But would it be necessary?

Over 19,000 fans were in attendance – roughly twice the season average – on a nervous day. Defender Tony James struck the only goal of the game in the first half and there were celebrations on the pitch once news arrived from Bath that Albion had drawn.

City may have begun the 1990s battling relegation to the old Third Division but they ended with the club on the verge of our seventh trip to Wembley in eight years.

Despite a successful decade on the pitch, tensions between fans and those in charge remained. One fanzine was provocatively titled Where's The Money Gone? Successive managers, Brian Little and Mark McGhee, became hated for the nature of their exits, although this was particularly tough on Little after achieving three visits to Wembley and promotion to the Premier League. Later, there were fierce protests against the so-called 'Gang of Four' board members: Gilbert Kinch, Roy Parker, Barrie Pierpoint and Philip Smith. For young fans otherwise lapping up own-brand Fox Leisure sportswear and motivational car bumper stickers, it felt like another fad dreamt up by the marketing department when fans handed out A3 paper outside the turnstiles. Kinch Out. Parker Out. Pierpoint Out. Smith Out. Collect the whole set.

And soon they were out, like Pleat and Shipman before them.

We had wanted the Gang of Four out mainly because of their clash with our manager, Martin O'Neill. Our whispered admission is that we had called for O'Neill's exit too during an infamous home defeat to Sheffield United just weeks after his arrival in March 1996. Hands up. We got that one wrong. He never let us forget it.

A bandy-legged young midfielder on loan from Chelsea made his debut against Sheffield United. From the top of the Carling Stand, a chant began. 'O'Neill out, Mustafa in…'

Mustafa became Muzzy. O'Neill became a hero. Leicester City became an established Premier League club, won the League Cup twice and played in Europe.

These were the glory years but we wanted more and there was a tantalising glimpse of a possible future in which City competed with the elite. Every fan of a certain age will tell you of one game in particular – a 5-2 home win against Sunderland inspired by a new strike partnership of Stan Collymore and Emile Heskey – which appeared to signal even greater times ahead. Within weeks, Heskey was sold to Liverpool. Within months, O'Neill was gone too and Collymore wasn't far behind. The club disintegrated.

For years, we looked back on that victory over Sunderland and wondered what might have been.

1: SUNDERLAND (H)

Saturday 8 August 2015

WHAT A GAME. WHAT A DAY. A DAY THAT BEGINS WITH THE England cricket team winning The Ashes just up the road and ends with Leicester City sitting top of the Premier League.

Cricket continues, but the ball that takes Australia's final wicket to seal victory in the Fourth Test at Trent Bridge before midday acts as something of a bookend to the summer sport. Just over three hours later, City open the 2015/16 Premier League season with a home fixture against Sunderland. Fans troop back to The Gateway, The Font, The Local Hero, The Robert Peel, The Counting House. Outside The Swan and Rushes, supporters of both clubs are sprawled on the pavement enjoying sunshine and heat that has been in short supply for some weeks.

Team news is keenly anticipated. The Japanese forward Shinji Okazaki will make his debut but the main talking point is the decision by new Leicester City manager Claudio Ranieri to switch from the effective 3-4-1-2 formation that helped bring survival at the end of last season to a more conventional 4-4-1-1.

The first one is Okazaki; the second is Jamie Vardy, playing his first competitive game since making his England debut in the summer. Kasper Schmeichel is the obvious choice in goal. The two banks of four read from right to left: Ritchie De Laet, Robert Huth, Wes Morgan, Jeffrey Schlupp; Marc Albrighton, Danny Drinkwater, Andy King, Riyad Mahrez.

As the players take to the pitch, the Kop is transformed into a gigantic graphic of two supporters – one with a scarf, one with a flag – made up of thousands of shiny foils held aloft in a display organised by fan group Union FS. At the front of the stand, a banner reads: 'Your colours are in our hands. Our dreams are in yours.'

Game on.

Sunderland start brightly, going close three times in the first ten minutes, but that only serves to make the next twenty even more painful for the thousands in red and white stripes in the away end. They have a good view of their team's abject surrender as City score three times to effectively end the contest before the half-hour mark.

Vardy gets the first, darting onto a Marc Albrighton free kick to loop a header up and over the giant frame of Costel Pantilimon with eleven minutes on the clock. He celebrates with a somersault, already one-fifth of the way to matching his total from last season.

Another arcing Albrighton cross is glanced in by Riyad Mahrez to double City's lead and Mahrez is soon taken down by Cattermole just inside the penalty area before placing the spot kick beyond Pantilimon.

3-0. We're up and singing now. Three points in the bag against one of our relegation rivals?

Lee Cattermole, Sunderland's captain and midfield lynchpin, is sacrificed after half an hour to make way for a second striker, the Scottish international Steven Fletcher, as Advocaat moves to 4-4-2. The veteran Dutch manager, persuaded by Sunderland to shelve impending retirement, has been bested by his opposite number. This is the first tactical victory of the season for Ranieri, who had been written off by large sections of the press after being appointed by City. Their chief gripe, that he was the polar opposite to his predecessor Nigel Pearson, is already shown up as under-thought nonsense just half an hour into a 38-game season.

Ranieri may act the fool occasionally in press conferences but he is a considered tactician. Mahrez, who had played centrally at the end of last season, is back on the wing rendering Sunderland's defensive midfielder redundant and replaced, instead tormenting left-back Patrick Van Aanholt to an extent that borders on cruelty.

The second half begins with more of the same. Vardy and Mahrez both create magnificent openings for themselves from tight angles but neither brings the fourth goal of the game. That eventually comes at the other end when a rare Sunderland attack sees Jermain Defoe find the corner of the net for his 129th Premier League goal.

The visitors are visibly buoyed and set off in pursuit of a second goal, only to concede yet again. This time it's Albrighton, albeit returning from an offside position, who takes advantage of slack play by Sunderland's new centre-back Younes Kaboul to fire past Pantilimon.

The Sunderland debutant Jeremain Lens then makes his first notable contribution of the match when he sets up Fletcher for a second consolation goal to offer brief hope for Advocaat's men. False hope, as it turns out. The three recent City purchases who had been enjoying the show from the bench – Christian Fuchs, N'Golo Kanté and Yohan Benalouane – all come on to help strengthen an increasing rearguard action by the home side. Vardy and Mahrez are withdrawn having given everything to establish the advantage.

The final whistle brings confirmation not only of victory but also City's status as Premier League leaders.

Fittingly, the key duel in the game sees one of Nigel Pearson's many astute signings completely dismantle one of Sven-Göran Eriksson's many indifferent ones. Mahrez has seen off better defenders than Sunderland's Van Aanholt, who was temporarily a City player when signed on loan by Eriksson in 2011, but few have given up with so little fight. Van Aanholt's lackadaisical approach to defending, often walking back to his position while City attack, is symptomatic of Sunderland's problem.

Frankly, City want it more. That's nothing new where the likes of Huth and Vardy are concerned, but we were keen to see how hard-working our arrival from the Bundesliga would be. The answer was emphatic. Shinji Okazaki slotted straight into the withdrawn striker role as though he had been playing in the Premier League for years, hassling opponents and setting up counter attacks in bustling fashion.

David Nugent, City's top scorer for three years running as we fought for promotion, is on the verge of completing a £4million move back to the Championship with Middlesbrough, and Okazaki's impressive debut plays a big part in reassuring City fans. Nugent may have been relegated to fifth choice by the signings of Okazaki, Leonardo Ulloa and Andrej Kramarić over the past twelve months, but his work rate could have been hard to replace. It is clear why the scouting team kept tabs on Okazaki for so long. He is the heir apparent to a popular player who proved effective in a winning team for many years.

City fans waking up to the exciting sight of our team sitting at the top of the Premier League table for the first time since October 2000 are soon brought crashing back to earth by a headline in *The Sun on Sunday*. Jamie Vardy has been filmed making a 'racial slur' in a casino in the early hours of a pre-season Sunday morning. It barely seems credible after the summer that Leicester City have been through, but the evidence is incontrovertible. Vardy uses the term 'Jap' repeatedly in reference to a Far Eastern man he is accusing of trying to see his cards. The nationality of his new strike partner adds to the plot line.

The tabloid exposé is a long tradition. It is hard to believe City didn't firmly 'remind their players of their responsibilities', to borrow a well-worn media relations phrase, after the farce in Bangkok. Vardy's misdemeanour merely causes them to repeat the message. There's never any question that one of City's most important players will meet the same fate as Tom Hopper, James Pearson and Adam Smith did in the summer. Vardy issues a swift apology and Ranieri confirms at his second pre-match press conference that there will be no sacking.

City, having been bumped off the top by Manchester City's win at West Bromwich Albion in the opening Monday night game of the season, prepare for a final ever trip to an unhappy hunting ground. Our first away game of the season takes us to Upton Park.

Leicester City 4 (Vardy, Mahrez 2, Albrighton)
Sunderland 2 (Defoe, Fletcher)
Team: Schmeichel, De Laet (Benalouane), Morgan, Huth, Schlupp, Mahrez (Fuchs), Drinkwater, King, Albrighton, Okazaki, Vardy (Kanté)

THE WILDERNESS YEARS

2002. AS AULD LANG SYNE RANG OUT FROM TINNY SPEAKERS across the East Stand into the night sky and the lights went out at Filbert Street for the last time, we tried to remember better days. For the older fans, that may have been Ken Keyworth's hat-trick against Manchester United. Some recalled Keith Weller's dancing tights of the seventies, the 5-0 play-off semi-final thrashing of Cambridge United in 1992 or Muzzy Izzet crashing a volley into the Tottenham Hotspur net on the night we pleaded for Martin O'Neill to stay in 1998.

In the end, O'Neill's departure was the catalyst for the club to implode and Filbert Street's last days were not happy ones. We looked forward to the future and the move to the shiny new Walkers Stadium just a wind-assisted goal kick to the south, but dark times were ahead. Soon we were meeting in backstreet pubs forming organisations to help save our club, shaking buckets outside home games and waiting anxiously for news. In the short term, Gary Lineker rode to our rescue with the help of his friends, Emile Heskey among them, as a group of local businessmen stumped up the cash to save our club. The 2002/03 season had seen the future of the club threatened but it ended with promotion.

In retrospect, that year feels like the odd one out. For a generation raised on the success of the O'Neill era, propped up by a return to the Premier League under Micky Adams, there wasn't much else to cheer about for the rest of the decade. Five years of gradual decline followed, during which we endured a high turnover of playing staff, uninspiring managers and poor football. Apathy set in and we became accustomed to our team facing similar clubs who were far better organised on and off the pitch. We had some memorable days, mainly when securing survival or battling to an unlikely FA Cup victory, but few chronicle these times because they're not worth reading about. This is the reality of football for most fans, but it's not glamorous and it's certainly not worth dwelling on.

We trudged our way towards the Britannia Stadium in May 2008 under the darkest of clouds, a fitting atmosphere for City's first-ever relegation to the third tier.

The players were a problem. Some of them didn't work hard enough. Others didn't possess the talent to merit wearing our shirt. A handful fitted into both categories. At times we didn't even recognise them, so often was the door revolving to bring in mediocrity and spit out failure. It was a similar issue with the number of managers that came in and out without achieving anything positive, although some had trying circumstances as a defence.

We had lost our identity. As we slipped out of the Championship for the first time, nearly eight years had passed since we last sang our hearts out to O'Neill's team. It felt like a hundred. Maybe we needed relegation and a rebuild.

Stoke fans danced in front of us, some seemingly celebrating our demise as much as their own promotion to the Premier League, and joining them felt like a very distant dream.

One of them approached.

'Heading back to Leicester? You want to go via Oldham, Swindon, Scunthorpe...'

We gave hollow laughs and stared straight ahead.

2: WEST HAM UNITED (A)

Saturday 15 August 2015

LAST CHRISTMAS, OR JUST ABOUT: 20 DECEMBER 2014. Leicester City left-back Paul Konchesky didn't give West Ham United his heart but he certainly gave them a present – the opening goal gift-wrapped for Andy Carroll to give the Hammers the lead in what had been an even game of few chances. Wham! Another kick in the ribs for Leicester City's travelling supporters.

It was the lowest point of Konchesky's season and one of many difficult moments for his team. So often City conceded the first goal, then a second, before a late, yet fruitless, rally.

As we sloped away from Upton Park with our team bottom of the league at Christmas, the home supporters skipped out of the exits with theirs in the Champions League places. It seemed inconceivable that the two sides would meet again in the league the following season.

Yet here we are. The sun beats down as stewards frantically clear claret and blue streamers from an immaculate playing surface and, against all the odds, Leicester City are back.

West Ham, buoyed by their win at the Emirates on the opening weekend, start brightly with Dimitri Payet, a £10.6million summer signing from Marseille, pulling the strings in midfield. In front of him, Diafra Sakho and Mauro Zarate run the channels to good effect. The home side go close when Wes Morgan sends a header narrowly over his own crossbar and the noise builds inside Upton Park in anticipation of an early goal.

Fortunately for City, it doesn't arrive. The tide begins to turn with Shinji Okazaki a revelation in the withdrawn striker role. He holds the ball up, links play and scurries back to win possession in midfield on numerous occasions.

Halfway through the first half, Vardy drops in behind West Ham centre-back Winston Reid to collect a ball from Marc Albrighton and looks up from the flank. He sees Okazaki's run and delivers a perfect cross into his strike partner's path. Okazaki meets the ball on the volley with the outside of his right foot, sending it towards goal. The save is made by Adrian but the Spanish goalkeeper can only push the ball up into the air. Leaping and hanging for a split-second, Okazaki nods it over the line for his first goal in English football. At the other end of the ground, we go wild.

Our team continues to impress. The same four attackers who tormented Sunderland are at it again and all four are involved in the goal that doubles City's lead. Vardy wins the flick on. Okazaki retrieves the ball and sets it back. Albrighton darts into the area and pulls it across to the edge of the area. Mahrez guides his finish disdainfully into the top corner of the net and hares off wearing the same gleeful expression as thousands in the away end. City are 2-0 up, having failed to win on any of our last 20 visits to the capital.

Just before half time, a long ball catches Huth and Morgan napping and leaves Sakho through on goal. The Senegalese striker lifts the ball past Kasper Schmeichel before falling to the floor inside the penalty area courtesy of the goalkeeper's outstretched right arm. It should be a penalty. It could be a red card. Again the fortune lies with City. Referee Anthony Taylor waves play on to the fury of the Hammers supporters.

The second half is a very different story. West Ham press forward and City retreat towards the edge of the penalty area. Payet quickly pulls a goal back with a neat finish into the top corner. City struggle to get out. Yet there are few shots to test Schmeichel. Ranieri makes similar defensive substitutions to the ones which helped close out the game against Sunderland, again introducing N'Golo Kanté, Christian Fuchs and Yohan Benalouane.

West Ham force one clear chance to equalise, working the ball to Sakho six yards out in the centre of the goal. He strikes the ball straight at Schmeichel who beats it away and both the chance and the game are gone. Leicester City have won in the league at West Ham for only the second time since 1966. We go top of the Premier League table for the second successive Saturday.

We're pinching ourselves as we leave Upton Park for the very last time. West Ham will move to the Olympic Stadium in Stratford when the season ends and another of English football's iconic stadiums will disappear. Visiting supporters will soon be able to tick off another new ground but we will lose the opportunity to visit the jellied eel shop on the Barking Road or Ken's Cafe which has served West Ham supporters for nearly fifty years. We won't see the bemusing sign above a dry cleaners on Green Street that reads: 'Don't Kill Your Wife, Let Us Do It!'

Upton Park has never been a happy hunting ground for Leicester City, but all football fans should treasure these grand old venues. At least we walked away for the last time having seen a City win.

West Ham United 1 (Payet)
Leicester City 2 (Okazaki, Mahrez)
Team: Schmeichel, De Laet (Benalouane), Morgan, Huth, Schlupp, Mahrez (Fuchs), Drinkwater, King, Albrighton, Okazaki (Kanté), Vardy

THE HARD ROAD BACK

THE MAN WHO CONDEMNED LEICESTER CITY TO THE LOWEST point in our club's history in the summer of 2008 was the man charged with restoring us to the Championship. Not Ian Holloway, whose last game was to be that goalless draw at Stoke, but Nigel Pearson, who had guided Southampton to safety at our expense.

Initially, we were underwhelmed. Thankfully, we were wrong. Pearson quickly assembled an honest, hard-working side that was far too good for League One and soon the club found itself back from whence it had arrived. We danced on Southend beach after Matty Fryatt's double secured the title and we trooped down Filbert Way the following Friday night to watch Matt Oakley lift our first trophy for nine years.

The football club felt fresh again, not least because there were exciting youth team players emerging. Andy King looked like an old head on young shoulders, while Max Gradel was tricky and skilful on the wing. Pearson had recruited well too, adding the likes of Jack Hobbs and Bruno Berner who were to prove equally comfortable in a higher division.

We had enjoyed League One. It had helped that we were winning most weeks, but it was a joy to visit new towns and new grounds. Some fans felt it was a disgrace that the club had been lowered to an unprecedented level but there were others who would miss places like Hereford, Scunthorpe and Yeovil. It felt more like proper football and our players, management and fans took it seriously. We were there because we deserved it and we left because we deserved it.

With that, it was back to the rigours of the Championship and another long, hard campaign that would bring us to the cusp of Wembley during a play-off semi-final second leg in Cardiff. When King's header found the corner of the net, we were so close. Then came a goal for Cardiff's Michael Chopra, Yann Kermorgant's infamous panenka and the sight of Martyn Waghorn lying on the ground and sobbing uncontrollably as Cardiff's players leapt over him to celebrate. There were tears in the away end too, a mixture of pride and disappointment. The young centre-back Jack Hobbs and veteran striker Steve Howard left the pitch with their arms draped around each other's shoulders, an image that seemed symbolic of the club's unity.

Yet again there was hope and yet again there was a wild change of direction that would throw us off course entirely.

Nigel Pearson left to join Hull City in mysterious circumstances at the end of the 2009/10 season, Paulo Sousa took his place and City began an ill-advised attempt to morph into Barcelona overnight. Suddenly, players who knew their roles inside out were expected to keep possession in tight areas. They looked unfit. The results were appalling. Sousa was never going to last long. And then came Sven.

The appointment of Sven-Göran Eriksson in October 2010 was, for a brief time, exciting. Here was a former England manager with a high-profile global reputation being given the opportunity to build a side at great expense. After the dreariness of the mid-2000s, it was no wonder that some fans gleefully threw themselves onto the bandwagon.

The Eriksson era had its moments. Some of the football was sublime, the high point being a glorious display at Pride Park that brought two wonderful goals by Yakubu and Andy King. It was never quite the right fit for the Championship though. Like some of his less prestigious predecessors, Eriksson signed too many players on loan and supporters perceived a lack of passion and commitment among the squad.

By November 2011, the Swede was gone too. The King Power consortium needed a capable man to steady the ship and begin to build for the future with a long-term plan. They needed Nigel Pearson.

Despite his previous success, fans were split. Eriksson had raised the club's profile from Pearson's spell in charge, if not its league position. Had we moved on? Would this be a step back?

It took Pearson a few months to adjust, but soon it felt like he had never been away. He signed Wes Morgan from Nottingham Forest; Danny Drinkwater from Manchester United; Jamie Vardy from Fleetwood Town. Finally we were seeing players with hunger, players with something to prove and players who showed their quality on a more consistent basis.

The 2012/13 season began with City playing exciting, attacking football and promotion to the Premier League appearing closer than at any point in the previous ten years. In mid-January, thousands of City fans packed into the away end at Ashton Gate and saw our side dismantle Bristol City with new signing Chris Wood scoring a hat-trick.

Few could have predicted the dismal run that followed. City collapsed from title favourites to be fighting just to make the top six. It took a last-minute winner at the City Ground – our first league away win against Nottingham Forest since 1972 – to secure a play-off place and spark delirium among the travelling supporters behind the goal.

The rollercoaster continued to Vicarage Road for a play-off semi-final second leg that would live as long in the memory as victory over Forest. Anthony Knockaert's penalty could have taken us to Wembley. Instead, it was saved and Watford raced up the other end where Troy Deeney's goal took us to the depths of despair. It hurt. It really hurt. It also felt like we would never get out of the Championship.

Luckily, our players had a stronger resolve than many of us realised and 2013/14 became one of our most glorious seasons. Perhaps driven on by the heartbreak of the previous campaign, the likes of Danny Drinkwater and Jamie Vardy improved to unimaginable levels. We cast our minds back to the mid-2000s and the roll calls of teams who had dominated the division, making a downtrodden City their cannon fodder along the way – Sunderland; Reading; Birmingham City. It was Leicester City's turn and we revelled in it.

Promotion was achieved on 5 April 2014 when Queens Park Rangers failed to beat Bournemouth. Lloyd Dyer's right-footed rocket at Bolton later clinched the title. Yet we had even greater celebrations in the weeks to come. We invaded the pitch at Huddersfield and mobbed Nigel Pearson and his players. Then we found ourselves standing in the centre circle after the final home game of the season, shielding our eyes against the sun as it dawned that we were finally back in the Premier League.

3: TOTTENHAM HOTSPUR (H)

Saturday 22 August 2015

AN UNBEARABLY HOT AND HUMID DAY RESULTS IN A GAME OF few chances between City and Tottenham Hotspur. Goals were expected but the first one doesn't arrive until the 81st minute. Harry Kane bustles through a crowd of City players and lays the ball off to Nacer Chadli, whose deep cross is headed into the net from close range by substitute Dele Alli. There are a number of defensive errors involved in the first opening goal conceded by Ranieri's men. Last season, City went a goal down on far too many occasions including ten of the first twelve games in all competitions. It has taken until the third game of the following campaign to concede first and a reaction is vital.

The ball is played back to Wes Morgan who looks to his right. Both Robert Huth and Ritchie De Laet are pointing further up the wing and Morgan obliges, launching one long into the Tottenham half. Jamie Vardy jumps early and wins the flick-on despite a height disadvantage.

The ball lands at the feet of Riyad Mahrez. He turns towards goal. This is where he thrives, running diagonally into the penalty area with the ability to go left or right. The defender, in this case the Tottenham centre-back Jan Vertonghen, always knows that Mahrez wants to cut inside on his left foot. But Mahrez did the opposite in the corresponding fixture last season, instead darting to the byline and pulling the ball across for Leonardo Ulloa to score.

The doubt is there, yet the left-back, Ben Davies, is still frantically pointing for Vertonghen to show Mahrez onto his weaker right foot. Davies knows what can happen if the man he has been marking all game gets a chance to shoot.

Mahrez is only able to engineer a quarter of a yard of space but that's enough. The ball rockets into the far corner with a ferocity rarely seen since his early days in a City shirt when a similar strike against Blackpool found the same side of the net.

The sight of six-foot-two Hugo Lloris diving full-length and yet still finding Mahrez's strike unstoppable is a sweet feeling for every fan who endured the Frenchman's string of improbable saves on Boxing Day last season to deny City a draw. Morgan should gain the ultimate revenge by securing all three points with a late point blank header but Lloris denies his fellow captain. The game ends one all.

This game is also notable for what happens just moments before the exchange of goals, with Gökhan Inler replacing Danny Drinkwater for his Leicester City debut.

Inler is the captain of Switzerland and the capture of such a prestigious player from Serie A club Napoli was one of the transfer window's most eye-opening deals.

Drinkwater and Andy King made it impossible for Ranieri to instate Inler from the beginning of his City career. Just as Nigel Pearson had needed to break up a successful midfield partnership when King and Dean Hammond made way for Esteban Cambiasso and Drinkwater after a few games of the previous season, Ranieri had to choose wisely when to introduce Inler and his fellow summer signing N'Golo Kanté.

Leicester City 1 (Mahrez)
Tottenham Hotspur 1 (Alli)
Team: Schmeichel, De Laet, Morgan, Huth, Schlupp, Mahrez (Ulloa), Drinkwater (Inler), King, Albrighton (Kanté), Okazaki, Vardy

THE BASEMENT BOYS

NIGEL PEARSON NEARLY RAN OUT OF TIME IN HIS FIRST FULL year as a Premier League manager.

The 2014/15 season began well. City looked competitive and made the best of a tough start to the fixture list, earning hard-fought draws against Everton and Arsenal. The problems began to mount when the time came to integrate star players, none of whom had featured in the impressive opening games, into a team functioning well in their absence.

By then, September's extraordinary 5-3 win over Manchester United seemed an anomaly rather than an indicator of the team's true potential. Jamie Vardy may have torn United to shreds that day but Riyad Mahrez was an unused substitute. And where did Esteban Cambiasso fit in? It took Pearson and his staff months to solve the conundrum of his team selection. The first time Vardy, Mahrez and Cambiasso all started the same game was the 0-0 draw with Sunderland at the end of November.

In the meantime, we suffered. The quartet of central midfielders employed in a narrow diamond formation in the 1-0 home defeat to West Bromwich Albion was a particularly low point in a difficult season, Mahrez again left to sit on the bench for the entire game. City were often set up to defend rather than attack, to build from a base that didn't actually exist.

When the great escape began, a consensus formed among the media that the performances had been good all season and ill fortune had played a large role in the team's inability to turn their potential into points. While this wasn't strictly true, there were periods within games when City looked unstoppable. That's what made it all the more frustrating.

There were beautiful moments along the way: The fightback at Anfield with Liverpool from two harshly awarded penalties to draw 2-2 on New Year's Day was remarkable; there were similarly inspired efforts in defeat at the Emirates and White Hart Lane.

As the players left the pitch following the 4-3 defeat by Tottenham Hotspur at the end of March, we resigned ourselves to relegation. They had given everything in that game. Everything. Only to be undone by a mixture of strong opposition, bad luck and questionable officiating.

We thought it was over.

4: AFC BOURNEMOUTH (A)

Saturday 29 August 2015

WHEN THE FIXTURES WERE RELEASED IN THE SUMMER, ONE STOOD out: a Bank Holiday weekend trip to the south coast – a nice break for the fans but business as usual for our players.

As Leicester City learned last season, the Premier League can be ruthless. Take your chances when you're on top, or prepare to pay the price. AFC Bournemouth were successors to City as Championship title winners and in their first two top flight games, they were handed lessons in the importance of the 'fine margins' that Nigel Pearson mentioned on so many occasions. The Cherries lost 1-0 against both Aston Villa and Liverpool despite playing well in both games.

Claudio Ranieri tweaks his starting line-up for the first time in the league for the trip to Bournemouth, giving N'Golo Kanté his full league debut in place of Shinji Okazaki to try to firm up the central midfield area.

City begin brightly and a borderline offside decision is all that denies Riyad Mahrez a fifth league goal of the season following a clever diagonal through ball from Marc Albrighton.

The impressive start fades though and Bournemouth start to dominate, switching the ball quickly to wide positions and encouraging their full-backs to overlap at every opportunity.

They get little joy down City's left with Albrighton tracking back well to help Jeff Schlupp. It's a different story on the other side of the pitch, where Bournemouth look dangerous. They're aided by a needless early booking for Ritchie De Laet and an early knock for Mahrez following a heavy challenge by former City winger Max Gradel in the opening moments of the game.

City look weak, with De Laet cautious and Mahrez struggling. When Mahrez loses the ball halfway inside City's half and a quick one-two is played around De Laet, both can only watch as Callum Wilson fires Bournemouth into the lead with an overhead kick.

The home side continue to push forward in search of a second goal and there's a let-off for City when referee Neil Swarbrick fails to spot that a Kanté foul on Leicester-born Lee Tomlin takes place just inside the area, awarding a free kick rather than a penalty.

At half time, we're relieved our side remains just one goal behind.

This fifteen-minute interval on the south coast marks the first grumblings of the Ranieri era, with right-back De Laet receiving criticism from many of the travelling fans. Mahrez is withdrawn, having had little attacking impact, Okazaki is introduced and Kanté moves out to the left side with Albrighton switching to the right.

Having swung one way and then the other through marginal decisions in the first half, the game is decided by a series of second half flashpoints. Bournemouth, having already lost left back Charlie Daniels to a knock picked up just before half time, are also forced to substitute both his replacement Tyrone Mings and the dangerous Gradel to serious injuries. There is no blame attached to City players for any challenges resulting in injury but the incidents help to ratchet up the tension inside a compact little stadium. That increases even further when Robert Huth thumps the ball at the prone Bournemouth striker Wilson from point blank range.

City are beginning to threaten the home side's goal as well as their top scorer's head. The attack comes mainly through the lightning pace of left back Schlupp.

Okazaki and Kanté, both typically busy out of possession, conspire to rob the ball and Kanté plays it to Jamie Vardy. He has been isolated for long periods but all it takes is one run and Vardy can change a game. So he hares off towards goal with three Bournemouth defenders in pursuit. From the visiting supporters' section, we get a perfect view of the deep breath Vardy takes before shifting his body weight and twisting his marker inside out.

Only one Bournemouth defender, the imposing Steve Cook, can catch City's rapid striker. Cook commits fully to the challenge, launching himself towards the ball. Of course, it's already gone. Vardy is sent tumbling to the turf, a sight we have seen so many times. Referee Swarbrick has had to make several difficult decisions throughout the game and there are even more yet to come, but this isn't one of them. This is as clear as day. Swarbrick points to the spot and we are jubilant.

Vardy takes the penalty himself, firing it high to Artur Boruc's left, before setting off towards us. A chaotic celebration ensues. Fans charge down the gangways and spill onto the pitch. In the stands, there are supporters dancing down the vacated rows. We see the same passion on Vardy's face that we saw at The Hawthorns and Turf Moor at the end of last season after vital second-half winners that helped the great escape to rumble on.

Eight minutes are added following the numerous injuries to Bournemouth players. Both sides have strong shouts for a penalty denied by Swarbrick following City's equaliser, but the game finishes one each. 1,500 City fans wedged into one corner of the Vitality Stadium are delighted with a point in the circumstances.

Jamie Vardy has saved the Bank Holiday weekend.

AFC Bournemouth 1 (Wilson)

Leicester City 1 (Vardy)

Team: Schmeichel, De Laet (Benalouane), Morgan, Huth, Schlupp, Mahrez (Okazaki), Drinkwater, King, Albrighton (Dodoo), Kanté, Vardy

THE GREATEST ESCAPE

IN THE 2014/15 SEASON, LEICESTER CITY – BOTTOM OF THE league table at the start of April – won seven of the last nine games to complete one of the most unlikely survival bids in the history of the top flight.

Winning the Championship had been fantastic but it was something else entirely to see our team perform on a stage witnessed globally by millions – and exceed everyone's expectations.

In the days following the final weekend of the season, there was a clamour to identify a single key factor that altered Leicester City's fate.

Despite the nerves, the tension and the uncertainty, there was unquestionably a growing momentum and belief from people on both sides of the advertising boards. On the pitch, there were key changes in formation, approach and personnel. Off the pitch, supporters responded and drove their team on. It all helped.

During a review of the season for Sky Sports, the former Arsenal and France striker Thierry Henry attributed City's upturn in form to one thing: 'putting the ball in the back of the net.' It wasn't as simple as that, but the display during the 2-1 defeat at the Emirates Stadium in February, which Henry said City should have won easily, is a good starting point for reflection.

At that time, our team was going down fighting. In fact, that night saw the first piece of the jigsaw fall into place with the debut of Robert Huth and a switch to three central defenders. The other big impression made at the Emirates was the counterattacking play of Jeff Schlupp and Riyad Mahrez, neither of whom were afraid to attack against one of the best teams in the league.

Nigel Pearson's defensive, 5-4-1 formation remained until a dour goalless draw with Hull in March, during which City played a more attacking 3-4-3. This seemed like a last chance thrown away but, with the benefit of hindsight, it was actually a vital point earned. Nikica Jelavić and Abel Hernandez both wasted glorious opportunities for the away side.

At the other end, we saw one striker rise to the challenge and another who wasn't quite ready for the demands of a Premier League relegation battle. In the dying embers of that game, Jamie Vardy's explosive pace in the inside-left channel was City's only attacking threat – in contrast to Andrej Kramarić's failure to attack a cross into the box.

Vardy, who had started as the central striker of a new-look front three against Hull, was pushed back out wide for the trip to Tottenham and Ulloa came in for Kramarić to play through the middle. This was the beginning of the late season redemption for two men who had not come close to recapturing the glory of the afternoon they had spent the previous September humbling the mighty Manchester United.

The 4-3 defeat at White Hart Lane at the end of March was another kick in the teeth but it also demonstrated City's ability to create chances and the need for Pearson to throw off the shackles to let his side attack more. It is hard to think anyone on board the team coach travelling away from the capital that day truly had faith that survival could be accomplished, but Esteban Cambiasso's defiant words suggested differently. Cambiasso's belief in his team-mates was another key factor that cannot be overlooked. As each of them raised their game, the Argentine began to resemble the conductor of an orchestra. And the noise began to swell. The celebrations that greeted Andy King's late winner against West Ham United represented the sound of City fans tuning up to roar our team home.

On the pitch, more missing pieces were added to the jigsaw. When City signed Marc Albrighton in the summer, the scouting department paid tribute to his almost unparalleled ability to create chances at Premier League level. They could not have foreseen that Albrighton would be a bit-part player for the vast majority of the season, nor could they have thought that his attacking qualities would be matched by impressive defensive work when he finally became a regular in the team.

Pearson, meanwhile, was tinkering with his formation all the time. He adapted it midway through the next two games, against West Bromwich Albion and Swansea City, and both changes earned victory – first switching to a 3-4-3 at The Hawthorns to go on the attack and snatch a win from behind, then reacting to Swansea's threat following an early City goal to play two banks of four and see the game out.

Nelson Oliveira should still have equalised for the Welsh side when one-on-one with Kasper Schmeichel. That moment neatly summarised two of the factors that contributed heavily to victory at Burnley in City's next game – the impact of Schmeichel's return to the side in vastly improved form and the importance of fine margins in deciding footballing fates. Schmeichel made two world-class saves at Turf Moor but dived the wrong way when Matthew Taylor struck his penalty towards the corner of the net. Taylor slipped as he hit the spot kick, the ball glanced the outside of the post and City struck the winner at the other end within a minute.

That minute, when everything went our way, was another catalyst for the growing belief. Three home games followed and not even defeat at the hands of Chelsea in the first could derail City's charge. Early goals were the order of the day against Newcastle and Southampton and neither side could recover. Different players were stepping up to the plate too: Leonardo Ulloa scoring twice against Newcastle and Riyad Mahrez matching that against Southampton.

Pearson's opposite numbers began to struggle from a tactical perspective. Newcastle's caretaker manager John Carver, who had been in the stands to watch Chelsea's masterclass, chose to ignore the lesson and played a narrow midfield which left acres of space for City's wing-backs. Schlupp and Albrighton were both at the peak of their powers and showed no mercy in their attacking play. Southampton enjoyed plenty of possession a week later but struggled to match City's intensity and Sadio Mane didn't enjoy the physical challenge posed by the imposing back three of Huth, Morgan and Wasilewski. He would thrive back home on the south coast seven days later when scoring the fastest hat-trick in Premier League history against Aston Villa, but he didn't like playing City one bit.

It was all becoming too much for the sides unlucky enough to be standing in the other half of the pitch at kick-off. Sunderland gave it a go but failed to break City down. Our Premier League survival was confirmed and the final game of the season was a five-star stroll in the park against Queens Park Rangers, a club in disarray.

So there was no single factor that turned City's season. Instead, it was a succession of marginal gains that saw survival secured and most of those could be filed under the heading of Nigel Pearson's ability to learn and develop under pressure.

That capability shown by Pearson didn't make for headlines in the same way that calling a journalist an ostrich did, but the end result was reported across the globe.

It was a winning run nobody predicted. City took 22 points from the last 27 available – more than any other team during the same period.

That the last game became meaningless given the perilous position two months earlier was remarkable. That the players still played like their Premier League lives depended on it was less so – Pearson demanded it.

Life went on. The players jetted off to the owners' homeland of Thailand. Jamie Vardy made his England debut against the Republic of Ireland in Dublin. New players were linked with moves to the club. Several out-of-contract players left. Nobody connected with Leicester City Football Club – players, staff, owners, supporters – would ever forget the greatest escape of all.

5: ASTON VILLA (H)

Sunday 13 September 2015

SEVEN MONTHS HAVE PASSED SINCE ASTON VILLA AND Leicester City played out a turgid FA Cup tie at Villa Park which deserved no goals rather than three. It was the day after Valentine's Day and one love affair was beginning as another looked to be coming to an end. Tim Sherwood sat in the stands plotting his charm offensive against the Villa faithful and Nigel Pearson stood with arms folded as large sections of the away end turned against him for the first time.

Sherwood's men were still playing as they had under previous manager Paul Lambert – plenty of pretty passing, very little end product – while Pearson and his players seemed to be running out of ideas and retreating into an increasingly defensive setup.

A half-time rallying cry from Sherwood galvanised Villa and they looked brighter after the break. Indeed, they looked like the club with more hope for the future with City bound for inevitable relegation. Of course, it didn't quite play out like that and Pearson's rediscovery of attacking without fear changed everything.

Villa limped into seventeenth place to seal their own safety but things had to change in the claret and blue half of Birmingham. Their two best players, Christian

Benteke and Fabien Delph, departed for the north west and Sherwood was handed the cash to rebuild. He was to end up competing with Pearson's successor, Claudio Ranieri, for many targets. Both clubs had their eye on France.

The more famous, established club won the tug-of-war to sign Nantes midfielder Jordan Veretout who opted for Villa Park despite a reported late bid from City. We settled for N'Golo Kanté.

Both Veretout and Kanté start on the bench as the two clubs renew acquaintances, while Okazaki returns to the starting line up and Gökhan Inler makes his full league debut.

City begin quickly but fail to get the goal. When the ball falls to Villa's newest young hope, Jack Grealish, on the edge of the box, he passes it into the corner of Schmeichel's net. City are behind for the third match in a row.

Ranieri changes things at half time, bringing off the ineffective Okazaki in favour of new loan signing Nathan Dyer who lines up on the right wing. Mahrez moves into the centre behind Vardy.

The England international is inches from an equaliser when his clever flick trickles just wide of Brad Guzan's near post following an explosive burst down the left from Schlupp. Vardy himself explodes past Joleon Lescott minutes later but the covering pace of Micah Richards denies a clear shot at goal.

City are preparing a double substitution when they fall further behind. Mahrez is robbed just inside the Villa half and Agbonlahor races along the touchline past Ranieri and the two waiting replacements before crossing for Carles Gil. The Spaniard takes it first time on his left foot, bending the ball past the outstretched dive of Schmeichel to send the away end wild with delight.

Twenty-five minutes remain. City's unbeaten start to the season looks to be coming to an end. Ranieri makes his changes: Ulloa and Kanté on for Albrighton and Inler. City revert to 4-4-2 with Mahrez moving back to the left, while Tim Sherwood removes the goalscorer Gil to send on Jordan Ayew on the Villa left.

Villa fans, intoxicated by their side's unexpected two-goal lead, are cheering every pass made by the visitors. Perhaps this is the catalyst City need. Within moments, Vardy is denied a penalty following excellent pressing by the substitute Kanté and yet another Schlupp run swiftly results in a corner. Mahrez's delivery finds Ritchie De Laet at the near post. A flick of the Belgian's boot and the ball crosses the line before it is cleared from underneath the crossbar by Ashley Westwood. Villa's lead is reduced to a single goal and the King Power rises to roar our team on in pursuit of a leveller.

Ranieri sees something: the Villa substitute Jordan Ayew has been slow to support his full-back as City attack down the right. Following the goal, Mahrez is switched across to that side in an attempt to take advantage.

The new recruit Nathan Dyer looks lively in possession and Kanté is tigerish in midfield. Villa's only hope is that time runs out before City's dominance tells. That hope is in vain and, as the former City striker Alan Smith says on his live Sky Sports co-commentary, Mahrez is the man.

The joint leading Premier League goalscorer picks up the ball just inside the Villa half. He turns Ayew with ease and heads for the edge of the box. No Villa player can get near him. He passes to Danny Drinkwater, who turns the ball across goal. Vardy's there, sliding in ahead of Bacuna and Richards.

It's in. 2-2. Let's go for more.

The only question now is whether Sherwood's men can hold on for a point, having been cruising to all three just fifteen minutes earlier. Their fans are silent. The momentum is palpable. With the home crowd buoyant and City's players vibrant, the 50/50s have become 70/30s. Only one team can win this. Only one team will win it.

We return to the talented young attacker Grealish whose goal put his side into the lead in the first half. He is having to defend in the 89th minute now, quite the other side of the coin but equally important as a top-level footballer. He has been left to attend to Mahrez, the man who has terrorised Villa for the entirety of the second half. Grealish takes one look at him, then another, and then he goes to press the ball, leaving the Premier League's most in-form player in space. Kanté doesn't hesitate. He just gives the ball to Mahrez.

Two remarkable things then happen.

Mahrez looks up and plays a sumptuous lofted through ball over the Villa back line to pick out a run from Dyer. It's delicate artistry from a player whose rapier thrusts and tricky twists have already turned Villa inside out. Guzan rushes out but he can't get there.

Dyer is brave, literally putting his neck on the line in an attempt to win City all three points. Guzan barrels straight into him but Dyer doesn't care. Not when he eventually gets to his feet to be informed by City physio Dave Rennie that he has just scored the winner on his debut.

City have done it. They've turned it around completely, achieving a breathless 3-2 win from two goals down. It's a brilliant victory for what is gradually becoming a brilliant team.

Ranieri punches the air with both fists. He and his players are roared down the tunnel by nearly 30,000 ecstatic home supporters. Leicester City are second in the

Premier League.
Leicester City 3 (De Laet, Vardy, Dyer)
Aston Villa 2 (Grealish, Gil)
Team: Schmeichel, De Laet, Morgan, Huth, Schlupp, Mahrez, Drinkwater,
Inler (Kanté), Albrighton (Ulloa), Okazaki (Dyer), Vardy

THE DEPARTURE LOUNGE

WE WERE STILL BASKING IN THE GLOW OF THE GREAT ESCAPE when we woke on the morning of 31 May 2015 to a report in the *Sunday Mirror* that made our hearts sink: three of Leicester City's young players – Tom Hopper, James Pearson and Adam Smith - had filmed themselves having sex with a number of women on a club visit to the Thai capital, Bangkok. One of the players was heard to make a racist remark about one of the women. The newspaper had obtained and released the shameful footage.

It was embarrassing for the club and humiliating for the owners.

The club conducted an investigation. More than two weeks passed before any decisive action was taken, the circumstances seemingly complicated by the family connection between James Pearson and his father – the City manager. During that period, the club's reputation took a battering. Eventually, the players were sacked.

A month on from the incident, Nigel Pearson was sacked too with the working relationship between manager and board said to be 'no longer viable.'

The positivity surrounding the King Power Stadium in the wake of the team's successful Premier League survival bid evaporated during June 2015. It had taken months and years of hard work from so many people to establish the club on a global stage and the actions of three young men to place everything in jeopardy.

The wait to discover Pearson's successor was tortuous. Day after day, new names appeared from across the wide spectrum of management: Guus Hiddink, Jürgen Klopp, Sean Dyche, Steve Cotterill, Predrag Radosavljevic.

Predrag who?

Radosavljevic - more widely known, although not that widely, as Preki – was the Serbian head coach of Sacramento Republic, a lower-league team in the United States. He had played for Everton and Portsmouth in the 1990s, but Preki was not a household name in England. Nor was Radosavljevic.

So when Sacramento called a press conference for Preki to announce he was leaving to take up a management job in the English Premier League, messageboards went into meltdown. Ours was the only vacancy. We panicked. Or we laughed hysterically. And we continued to wait.

Preki never arrived. He didn't seem to go anywhere at all – vanishing into thin air but remaining a mysterious footnote in the history of Leicester City Football Club.

The man who did arrive, holding up our blue shirt for the cameras with a genial smile, was Claudio Ranieri, seven months after losing his job as manager of the Greek national team following defeat to the Faroe Islands.

Perhaps we were exhausted after a gripping Premier League season followed by a damaging summer for the club but the general reaction among supporters was apathy, perhaps tinged with relief that the saga had been concluded.

Everything seemed to move slowly that summer: two weeks for the players to be sacked; another two weeks for the manager to go; another two weeks for his successor to be named. Ranieri had only three weeks before the first Premier League fixture of the season to get to know his new players.

There was plenty to do. At first, however, Ranieri did very little. He stood on the sidelines watching his new squad at a training camp in Austria and took it all in.

Even in pre-season, a time to experiment, we didn't see many changes: Ranieri fielded the same 3-5-2 formation that had brought Pearson success and the players continued to play with the energy and commitment that characterised the great escape.

When Pearson left, we feared those players who had fought for him in the final weeks of the season would disband and Leicester City would have to start from square one.

We were delighted our influential assistant managers, Craig Shakespeare and Steve Walsh, stayed at the club.

We were concerned when the influential Esteban Cambiasso left, relieved when Gökhan Inler arrived to replace him and intrigued to see how other summer signings from across Europe would fare: Shinji Okazaki from Mainz in the German Bundesliga, Yohan Benalouane from Atalanta of the Italian Serie A and N'Golo Kanté from Caen in the French Ligue 1.

There were new faces but in the first few weeks of the season, Claudio Ranieri was praised to the hilt for how little he wanted to change as City started the season in terrific form.

6: STOKE CITY (A)

Saturday 19 September 2015

IN MAY 2008, DEFEAT AT STOKE SAW LEICESTER CITY FOOTBALL Club sink to the third tier of the English game for the first time in our history. The next time we visited the Britannia Stadium, in September 2014, we won in the Premier League for the first time in over ten years.

What would the 2015 edition of this fixture bring?

Claudio Ranieri uses his pre-match press conference to extend an offer of free pizza to his players if they are able to keep their first clean sheet of the season.

N'Golo Kanté returns to the starting line up in place of Marc Albrighton on the left in City's only change. Unfortunately, there is only one team in the game during the first 45 minutes and they're not wearing blue. City can't cope with the movement and invention of Stoke's creative trident of Marko Arnautović, Bojan and Xherdan Shaqiri. It comes as no surprise when Arnautović gets the better of Ritchie De Laet and plays in Bojan for a simple finish to put the hosts into the lead.

City have fallen behind for the fourth match in a row. We've come back in the previous three but this is the first time we go 2-0 down before half time. An innocuous long ball should be dealt with comfortably by either the former Stoke centre-back Robert Huth or City captain Wes Morgan. Instead, Huth lets the ball drop and Morgan makes a mess of a simple backpass. Jonathan Walters nips in to beat Kasper Schmeichel.

Stoke have the chance to go further ahead before the break but Ranieri's men hold on and it says much about the credit they have already built up with their superb start to the season that the away end roars them down the tunnel at half time with a positive rallying cry. These players and fans have been through a lot together and we share an understanding and respect. Now let's get back into this.

Gökhan Inler, ineffective during a ponderous first half, is replaced by Albrighton with Kanté moving into the centre, but it's the other two midfielders who soon combine to force an error. Danny Drinkwater plays a one-two with Riyad Mahrez and advances into the box. Drinkwater feels pressure from the retreating Arnautovic who pushes the City man to the ground. Mahrez sweeps the resulting penalty into the corner of the net and the comeback is on.

City are a team transformed and Kanté in particular is a man possessed, charging around midfield with a fiery urgency and robbing the ball with impressive regularity.

Drinkwater launches a high ball forward. Mahrez nips in from the wing to win the flick-on ahead of both Stoke centre-backs, leaving Jamie Vardy to race clear through on goal. We feel a sense of déjà vu. Vardy through on goal in front of a packed away end in the West Midlands? There are shades of the winners at St Andrew's and The Hawthorns in the previous two seasons as England's number nine steadies himself.

As at West Bromwich Albion five months ago, Vardy is on his weaker foot. Not such a clean connection. The same corner of the net though, and City have staged an unlikely comeback for the fourth game in a row.

Both sides have chances to win it. Stoke defender Geoff Cameron sends a header inches wide and Vardy fires an injury-time shot just past the post at the other end. It remains 2-2 at the final whistle though, and we end the weekend in fourth place in the Premier League.

No clean sheet and still no pizza for City's porous back line, but plenty of entertainment from one of the most thrillingly attacking teams in the country.

The following Tuesday evening, the unbeaten run continues and so does City's involvement in the League Cup. A reserve side made up of several players yet to start a league game wins an entertaining home tie against West Ham United in extra time. Just four minutes away from a penalty shootout, Andy King heads the winner at the Kop end. There are ten changes to the starting line up from the Stoke game, with Gökhan Inler the only player to retain his place in a bid to improve the Swiss international's match fitness.

So many members of the team marked 'Plan B' impress and Ranieri may have some re-categorising to do for the weekend's visit of Arsenal. Of those yet to begin a league match, the standout performers are left-back Christian Fuchs, whose pin-point deep cross finds King for the winner, Yohan Benalouane at centre-back and Leonardo Ulloa at centre-forward.

Shinji Okazaki's workrate has endeared him to City fans but he has shown little since his classy contribution to the first two wins of the season. Ulloa's substitute appearances have grown increasingly assured and now the question is whether the Argentine can force his way into Ranieri's thoughts for the visit of Arsenal. It was Ulloa's equaliser that earned City a point in the same fixture last season.

N'Golo Kanté is fast becoming a fans' favourite for his incredible ability to reclaim possession in midfield. West Ham fielded a strong team but the turning point could have arrived at 1-1 with Dimitri Payet's introduction. Payet has, along with Mahrez, been one of the best players in the league so far this season. Yet Kanté barely gives him a sniff. Mahrez is winning the headlines but there are murmurs in the stands about Kanté as well. His energy. His pace. His formidable tackling. These are the murmurs you hear when football fans are watching someone truly special.

Stoke City 2 (Bojan, Walters)
Leicester City 2 (Mahrez, Vardy)
Team: Schmeichel, De Laet, Morgan, Huth, Schlupp, Mahrez, Drinkwater,
Inler (Albrighton), Kanté (King), Okazaki (Ulloa), Vardy

THE PREDICTIONS

THE COVER OF THE DAILY MAIL'S PREMIER LEAGUE SEASON preview featured a close-up portrait of José Mourinho, alongside a quote from Jamie Carragher that read: 'Why this man is worth ten more points than any other manager.'

Sixteen journalists and former footballers were invited to give their predictions. All sixteen gave the same top four in varying orders: Chelsea, Arsenal, Manchester City, Manchester United. Fifteen said Chelsea would win the league, with a sole vote for Manchester City.

Ten said Leicester City would be relegated.

The BBC's chief football writer Phil McNulty predicted Leicester to finish 19th, saying: 'The appointment of Claudio Ranieri means I fear the worst.'

Seven of the eleven *Guardian* writers to offer their predictions picked Chelsea to win the title, with two votes apiece for Arsenal and Manchester City.

Nine picked Leicester to be relegated, including Daniel Taylor who highlighted Nottingham Forest's exploits in the 1970s as 'the kind of implausible success story that could never happen again.'

Even former Leicester players expected a season of struggle. In the *Daily Telegraph*, Alan Smith predicted an 18th-placed finish. Robbie Savage's forecast in the *Daily Mirror* put Leicester 17th.

We've started well.

Let's see.

7: ARSENAL (H)

Saturday 26 September 2015

THE WEEK LEADING UP TO ARSENAL'S VISIT IS PUNCTUATED BY reminders of what could have been. Leicester City are fourth in the Premier League table, above Arsenal and the champions Chelsea. Flick to the next table and you find the three relegated sides from last season, one of which looked certain to be City for so long.

On Monday, Burnley travel to Derby County for a televised Championship clash which is talked up beforehand but offers zero entertainment value, zero goals and not much in the way of atmosphere either. On Wednesday, City are drawn to face Hull – the side who ultimately suffered relegation as a result of the greatest escape – in the next round of the League Cup. On Friday, Queens Park Rangers are thumped 4-0 by neighbours Fulham in another televised Championship match.

These events will pass most City fans by, but some of us are still pinching ourselves at our Premier League status and the opportunity for our team to test itself against the likes of Arsenal.

The Arsenal manager, Arsène Wenger, is an anomaly in the modern game. The famous 3-3 draw at Filbert Street feels like a lifetime ago. In fact, it was September

1997 when Dennis Bergkamp scored one of the greatest hat-tricks in English football and City still managed to fight back to level the match. So much has changed since then but Wenger will again take his position in the opposing dugout, this time a few hundred yards to the south west.

Given City's current propensity to score, concede and come back from a losing position, another six-goal thriller doesn't seem impossible.

As it turns out, a comeback looks so unlikely with ten minutes to play that fans are streaming out. City trail 4-1 as Arsenal's Chilean superstar Alexis Sánchez turns a close encounter of the open kind into an extra-terrestrial display of forward play and finishing power. Jamie Vardy soon scores the sixth goal of the game to become the leading scorer in the Premier League but Olivier Giroud notches the seventh in injury time and Arsenal run out 5-2 winners.

City must have felt encouraged initially by a bright start and a superb opening goal. Kanté won a trademark tackle in his own penalty area and his midfield partner Danny Drinkwater launched a magnificent long pass to the left where Vardy had peeled off Per Mertesacker. Vardy's header expertly cushioned the ball into his path and he had the beating of Mertesacker for pace. That wasn't surprising in the slightest but eyebrows were raised at the ease with which he finished past Petr Čech, firing hard to the Arsenal goalkeeper's left into the far corner of the net from a narrow angle. It was a brilliant goal and one befitting an England international striker.

Sadly for City, Arsenal's own lightning fast England forward, Theo Walcott, rolled in an equaliser seven minutes later from a swift counter attack after a Vardy header hit the bar at the other end.

Then Sánchez took over. His first was routine, his second was a header from a pinpoint lofted pass by Mesut Özil and his third was a superb low drive from distance that beat Kasper Schmeichel's outstretched hand.

So City's unbeaten start to the season comes to an end in the face of a masterclass in pass-and-move football from an excellent side. It's an understandable fate but nobody enjoys watching their team concede five – all a far cry from Ranieri's pre-match patter about pizza.

The question now is whether the tinkering should begin. Ten of the eleven that started against Arsenal were also present in the opening day line up and there are players pushing for inclusion in the next outing at Carrow Road. Should Christian Fuchs, impressive in the League Cup win over West Ham, come in for Jeff Schlupp at left-back? Should Yohan Benalouane be accommodated in the backline? Is there a place in attack for Leonardo Ulloa given the travails of Shinji Okazaki in recent weeks? These are all questions that Ranieri must ponder in the face of City's first defeat of the season.

Leicester City 2 (Vardy 2)
Arsenal 5 (Walcott, Sanchez 3, Giroud)
Team: Schmeichel, De Laet, Morgan, Huth, Schlupp, Mahrez, Drinkwater
(Kramarić), Kanté, Albrighton (Ulloa), Okazaki (King), Vardy

THE SCHOOL OF SCIENCE

LEICESTER CITY'S PLAYERS LEAVE THE FIELD SHATTERED AFTER giving everything against Arsenal. It will be two weeks until they take to the field again in the Premier League but with the majority of the squad setting off around the world to play international games, recovery will be vital.

We've got that covered.

Perhaps the greatest legacy left by Nigel Pearson is the cutting-edge medical and sports science departments that have helped to revolutionise Leicester City Football Club.

When Ranieri took over as manager, he was astonished by the level of detail behind the scenes.

These key staff provide everything the players need to achieve success and their names have become well-known among supporters: Paul Balsom, Head of sports science and performance analysis; Andrea Azzalin, First-team science and conditioning coach; Matt Reeves, Head of fitness and conditioning; Mitch Willis, Strength and power coach; Dave Rennie, Head physiotherapist.

Fascinating insights into the work of these departments are carefully disseminated through the media – cryotherapy chambers to aid recovery; GPS tracking to manage the players' fitness; the positive effects of beetroot juice on performance – and we lap it up. It's reassuring to know that no stone is left unturned in pursuit of success.

Of course, supporters don't need to see every detail. It's all about trust, built through those stories about the positive effect of sports science. Just as we can trust our players to give full effort and commitment in each game, we know they could not have been better prepared before they take to the pitch.

The results are clear: Leicester City players don't get as many injuries as those from other clubs.

In their 5-2 triumph at the King Power, Arsenal may have won the battle. Leicester City's school of science could help win the war.

8: NORWICH CITY (A)

Saturday 3 October 2015

THE T-SHIRT WEATHER AND FEEL-GOOD FACTOR OF AUGUST should feel a long time ago now. Reality must surely kick in soon. Yet, as we make the horizontal trek east to Norfolk, the sun is out and there remains a positive outlook in the away end despite the prospect of a tricky fixture to follow defeat against Arsenal.

Norwich have adapted well after promotion to the Premier League, having retained several players from their previous season in the top flight. They favour possession-based football, which should play perfectly into City's hands with the counter attack a constant danger.

The big news ahead of kick-off is Claudio Ranieri's decision to drop Riyad Mahrez from the starting line up. Mahrez has not only been City's star man so far this season but one of the most impressive players in the country. He is the leading points scorer in the official Fantasy Premier League game. If few City fans can understand Mahrez's omission, even fewer of the thousands of fantasy managers across the world to transfer him into their team can believe their eyes.

In truth, it's entirely understandable. Ranieri is desperate to provide City with a more solid foundation upon which to build their counter-attacking style, particularly away from home. Mahrez, while brilliant on the ball, has frequently been lacklustre when called upon to defend. Jeff Schlupp moves up to the left wing, Marc Albrighton starts on the right and Christian Fuchs slots in at left back for his first league start with Danny Simpson coming in at right back.

Norwich manager Alex Neil has omitted his own flying winger, the dangerous Nathan Redmond, as both managers take a pragmatic approach.

City take a while to grow into the game but it's worth the wait. After coping with an initial flurry of activity from the home side, the visitors seize control of midfield and begin to fashion opportunities. It's no surprise when we score.

N'Golo Kanté cuts out a through ball and sends one of his own in behind the Norwich back line. Jamie Vardy nips in front of Sebastian Bassong, who takes the bait. Vardy tumbles to the floor under minimal contact and referee Mark Clattenburg points to the spot. With Mahrez off the pitch as he was at Bournemouth when Vardy stepped up to equalise, City's striker takes the responsibility again. Vardy thumps the ball into the net.

City aren't content to sit on the opening goal. The attacking raids continue, led by Albrighton's darting runs down the right side and the industry of Vardy and Shinji Okazaki. Schlupp and Albrighton both come close to doubling City's lead but neither makes contact with the ball. Okazaki repeatedly eludes the attentions of his marker but is unable to test Ruddy. What City need is a fierce strike to establish a two-goal cushion and ease any lingering nerves in the away section. Step up Jeff Schlupp.

Two minutes into the second half, Okazaki and Schlupp combine to win possession halfway inside their own half and the latter sets off across the centre circle. There are runners left, right and centre. Schlupp, often at his best when acting instinctively, thankfully picks the correct option on this occasion, sending the ball left. Kanté collects it and cuts inside before directing a clever return pass to Schlupp. City fans have seen our exciting young Academy product in this position so many times, usually resulting in opposition goal kicks, but Ruddy will soon be collecting the ball from the back of the net rather than retrieving it from the crowd. Schlupp dummies momentarily before firing into the far corner.

There is great joy on the faces of the celebrating players heading towards the away end. Norwich manager Alex Neil speaks afterwards of his exasperation at conceding a goal from a counter attack, a situation he specifically prepared his players to face. This is a great moment for Ranieri. Even when the opposition manager knows what's coming, there's nothing he can do to stop it. This is the third game in a row in which a ball has gone from back to front quickly and ended up in the opposition net. This is City's best counter attack yet, all the more impressive for not having involved Vardy or Mahrez at all.

Norwich have no option but to push forward even more in search of a way back into the game and what follows is greater possession for the hosts and opportunities for City on the break. None are taken and Norwich substitute Dieumerci Mbokani's consolation goal means a nervy finale but the game ends 2-1.

Still no clean sheet. We don't care. City are another three points closer to whatever the aim might be this season. Ranieri insists that his target remains survival, but his side head into the international break in fifth position having collected 15 of the 40 points probably needed for safety from just eight games. On the long journey west away from Carrow Road, City fans are looking up rather than down.

Norwich City 1 (Mbokani)

Leicester City 2 (Vardy, Schlupp)

Team: Schmeichel, Simpson (Benalouane), Morgan, Huth, Fuchs, Albrighton, Drinkwater, Kanté, Schlupp (King), Okazaki (Ulloa), Vardy

THE FUTURE OF THE LEFT

10 OCTOBER 2009. LEICESTER CITY'S UNDER 18 TEAM ARE PLAYING against Tottenham Hotspur at the club's Belvoir Drive training ground. Tottenham's youngsters, including a 16-year-old Harry Kane just three months into a scholarship contract, lead 2-0 at half time. The young Foxes fight their way back into the game and the tables are turned. It's 3-2 to the team in blue.

In the dying minutes, a powerfully built City left-winger receives the ball and starts to sprint. The assembled onlookers have seen him do this before but the Tottenham players look startled. It's nearly the end of the match. How is he doing it? This isn't any old sprint. This kid looks like a hundred-metre runner. He motors down the wing and crosses the ball to create a fourth goal for his team.

Some goals are scored in slow motion. This one is scored in fast forward.

Jeff Schlupp will score a hat-trick on his debut as a striker.

Sven-Göran Eriksson will try to convert him into a left-back.

Schlupp will play a key role at left wing-back in Leicester City's great escape under Nigel Pearson.

Claudio Ranieri will restore him to the left wing where he first wreaked havoc on the training pitches at Belvoir Drive.

Jeff Schlupp is the future of the left.

9: SOUTHAMPTON (A)

Saturday 17 October 2015

LEICESTER CITY AND SOUTHAMPTON HAVE FOLLOWED A similar path over the past two decades. Both were Premier League clubs in the late 1990s. Both dropped down to the Football League for periods at the beginning of the twenty-first century. Both made it as far down as League One before they began their revivals. It took City longer to get back to the top flight and Southampton have been viewed as a model club in recent years.

Southampton have done everything right: developed their Academy players, sold them for gigantic fees and spent that money well to continuously improve. The only problem they, along with the likes of Swansea and Stoke, have now is what happens next. The biggest clubs in the country are so well-established at the top of the Premier League table that Saints fans must be asking themselves whether this is as good as it gets.

Perhaps it's the virtually identical stadia, designed by the same firm of architects, that convinces City fans our club can reach the same level as the Saints.

There was a time, around ten years ago, that the long trip to the south coast would always result in defeat to an impressive Southampton side and there would be a deafening roar from the Itchen and Northam stands either side of a gloomy away end.

It's certainly too early to say City are operating at Southampton's level as we make the trip again but the Itchen and Northam don't seem as boisterous as they once did and it doesn't feel like the visit to St Mary's will end in the predictable 2-0 defeat it did last season.

Leicester City are unrecognisable from the side that fell to two late Shane Long goals that day, but remain unchanged from the win at Norwich. That means Riyad Mahrez takes his place on the bench once more. He won't stay there all afternoon.

City start well and the home fans are showing signs of nerves, yet there is no early goal to accompany the bright football and it isn't long before Saints begin to assert their authority in midfield. Danny Drinkwater and N'Golo Kanté chase shadows. The hosts manage to turn their spell of dominance into a 2-0 half-time lead despite creating very little from open play, both goals coming from set pieces.

It's a world away from the Martin O'Neill years when Arsène Wenger described City as the best team in Europe at corners and free kicks. These days, we look vulnerable from any well-taken dead ball. Southampton take plenty of good set pieces. They're a tall side. The pairs of centre-backs on each team mark each other leaving their 6 foot 4 inch centre-forward Graziano Pellè to be marked by 5 foot 10 inch City right-back Danny Simpson. No, City are not tall and we pay the price.

The first goal sees José Fonte make a run to the near post, easily eluding his marker Wes Morgan, to head into the far corner. Kasper Schmeichel is motionless.

The second should be flagged offside but the linesman allows Virgil Van Dijk to stand beyond the last line of defence and tap in at the second attempt following a flick-on by Pellè.

Claudio Ranieri introduces Mahrez and Nathan Dyer at half time in place of Jeff Schlupp and Shinji Okazaki. Mahrez will play behind Jamie Vardy with Dyer on the right and Marc Albrighton moving to the left.

Yet again, Ranieri's half-time tinkering works wonders. Mahrez gets on the ball straight away and begins to make things happen. Dyer causes havoc. Most importantly of all, Jamie Vardy grows into the game having been marshalled well by Fonte and Van Dijk before the interval.

Halfway through a second half dominated by City, Vardy strikes to spark jubilant scenes behind the goal. It's the sixth consecutive Premier League game in which he has scored. Dyer beats Van Dijk on the right and sends a perfect cross to the near post where Vardy gets between two men to power a header past Kelvin Davis from close range.

Spurred on by an away end packed with belief, City continue to plug away in search of an equaliser. One superb move ends with a Mahrez pull-back being fired over the top by Vardy's weaker left foot.

The goal is coming though. It has to come.

A poor clearance by Davis is controlled well by Drinkwater who moves the ball forward. Dyer moves in from the flank to scrap for possession and move it on again. Mahrez takes it up. Vardy anticipates the next pass and peels off his marker. Mahrez times the through ball to perfection and releases Vardy, just as he did at Birmingham and Barnsley during City's Championship-winning season.

The combination of two talented attacking players showing their best qualities is what it takes to undo Southampton. Vardy's acceleration takes him away from the Saints defence and he rockets the ball past Davis.

The comeback kings have done it again.

Southampton 2 (Fonte, Van Dijk)

Leicester City 2 (Vardy 2)

Team: Schmeichel, Simpson, Morgan, Huth, Fuchs, Albrighton, Drinkwater, Kanté, Schlupp (Dyer), Okazaki (Mahrez), Vardy

THE AUSTRIAN FOX

CHRISTIAN FUCHS QUICKLY BECAME A FAVOURITE WITH Leicester City fans after his arrival at the club in the summer of 2015.

City needed an assured, dependable Premier League left-back and it seemed too good to be true when the captain of the Austrian national team turned up on a free transfer from Bundesliga side Schalke 04. We were getting a natural leader as well as an accomplished footballer with Champions League experience.

It took a few games for Fuchs to force his way into the starting line up but there was no stopping him once he came in for the trip to Norwich in October. He soon became one of the first names on the team sheet each week, combining whole-hearted effort with a wand of a left foot and a monstrously long throw.

The real basis of the bond Fuchs has forged with City fans lies off the pitch with his social media presence. Where so many footballers' official Facebook, Twitter and Instagram accounts seem to coldly promote their 'brand' or exist solely as a vehicle to trot out the same tedious messages after every game, Fuchs is a breath of fresh air. He just wants to have fun.

So we've followed his cheeky hashtag, #NoFuchsGiven, with interest as he has posted short videos of quirky contests with Robert Huth, Jamie Vardy and Shinji Okazaki. Who doesn't want to see Huth power a football at his team-mate's backside, Vardy crack an egg over his forehead or Okazaki get a clip round the ear in the club canteen?

It's all in the name of entertainment for younger fans and the tabloid media also love it. Fuchs reflects the ease with which the whole club has adapted to a new level. He is the ultimate professional and he appears to see his responsibility as a footballer extending beyond his duties each match day to engage with supporters online.

As a bonus, Christian Fuchs is also one of the best left-backs ever to play for Leicester City Football Club.

10: CRYSTAL PALACE (H)

Saturday 24 October 2015

JAMIE VARDY STANDS IN THE CORNER OF THE KING POWER
Stadium and counts his fingers.

One. Two. Three.

It's difficult to count when Danny Drinkwater is jumping on your back.

Four. Five. Six.

It's noisy too. We make a hell of a racket.

Seven. Eight. Nine.

Running out of fingers.

Ten.

Ten Premier League goals in ten games and Jamie Vardy is the match-winner for Leicester City yet again.

Not only that, but it's another brilliant goal.

The giant Norwegian centre-back Brede Hangeland helped Crystal Palace to a 1-0 win at the King Power Stadium last season with a succession of towering headers to thwart increasingly desperate long-ball football from City. This time he's largely responsible for his side's 1-0 defeat. That said, there is still plenty to do even after

Hangeland miscontrols close to the halfway line.

The ball bounces loose to Riyad Mahrez, restored to the starting line up after two games. Mahrez could take a touch but instead he opts to play the ball first time on the volley, a difficult skill given the wet turf that has seen most of the afternoon's through balls scoot past their intended target. If anyone can do it, Mahrez can.

Vardy is already on the half-turn. Hangeland is taken out of the equation and his central defensive partner Scott Dann is left to deal with the Premier League's top scorer racing towards Wayne Hennessey in the Palace goal.

Hennessey hares out but can only watch as Vardy delicately lifts the ball over him. Now all Vardy has to do is get to the ball before Dann. Given that only one defender, Arsenal's Hector Béllerín, has matched City's front man for pace all season, not even the Palace fans are backing Dann to win this race. Vardy gets there first and smashes the ball high into the roof of the empty net.

The players return to their positions for Palace's restart. It had been a tight game until Hangeland's slip and remains one of those edgy encounters that really drive home the thin line between success and failure at the highest level of professional sport. Palace have two strong penalty appeals turned down by referee Mike Dean in the closing stages. Either one could have been given, but instead Christian Fuchs is given the benefit of the doubt on both occasions.

On the touchline, Claudio Ranieri whirls his arms and implores the crowd to raise the noise levels.

We respond and it helps. More than six months have passed since the King Power Stadium last greeted the final whistle of a league game with a roar of sheer relief. There have been plenty of victories in that time, one draw and a couple of defeats, but nothing like the late Palace rally that could have stolen away two precious points. In his post-match interview, Ranieri calls it ten English minutes at the end of an Italian tactical encounter.

Either way, City's multinational back line holds out to ensure their side moves onto 19 points after just ten games. To put this achievement into context, it took City 29 games to reach 19 points in the previous season. It's hard to believe that a relegation battle will ensue at any stage now, never mind the kind of escapades that became necessary earlier in 2015. Incredibly, we have the same number of points when the clocks go back as we did when they went forward in the previous season.

Since City's great escape began on Saturday 4 April 2015, no team has won more league points. October 2014 to April 2015: worst team in the Premier League. April 2015 to October 2015: best team in the Premier League.

Does it get any better than this?

Leicester City 1 (Vardy)
Crystal Palace 0
Team: Schmeichel, Simpson, Morgan, Huth, Fuchs, Albrighton (Okazaki),
Drinkwater, Kanté, Schlupp, Mahrez (Dyer), Vardy

THE INCONVENIENCE OF IT ALL

ON TUESDAY 27 OCTOBER, A MUCH-CHANGED CITY SIDE EXIT
the League Cup at Hull City's KC Stadium after a penalty shootout. The match sees
promising youngster Ben Chilwell make an assured debut at left-back. Riyad Mahrez
scores in extra time but then misses the opening spot kick of the shootout to send
City out of the competition after all five Hull players hit the target from twelve yards.
One of the most striking differences about life as a Premier League supporter when
compared to the Football League is that lots of fans appear to hate football.

It often seems as though they would be happier to forego matches entirely, so
concerned are they about fixture congestion or injuries to star players or lack of focus
on the most important competitions or the fact another team might beat them, or
not beat them, or even, heaven forbid, take them to a replay.

Some fans are desperate for the league table to reflect the order of wage bills, from
highest to lowest, or want European qualification to be dependent on money, like a
sign at a theme park. If you didn't spend £49million on your right-winger, you can't
go on the ride.

Leicester City have come from the unrelenting slog of the Championship into this
strange new world in which many matches in the football calendar are viewed as an
inconvenience.

Wes Morgan didn't have a summer holiday worthy of the name, instead playing in two
tournaments with Jamaica before returning for pre-season with City. He never complains.

Yes, Claudio Ranieri fields an entirely different team in the League Cup and FA Cup
to the one he uses in the Premier League – a decision that is decried by the media and
also some City fans. But this is common sense, the kind of clever management that we
will look back upon later in the season and applaud.

It helps to keep fringe players fresh and gives them the chance to stake a claim to
be involved in league fixtures. N'Golo Kanté and Christian Fuchs both demonstrated
their talent in League Cup games before being assimilated into Ranieri's Premier League
line-up.

City fans are disappointed to exit the League Cup, but perhaps we have bigger fish
to fry.

11: WEST BROMWICH ALBION (A)

Saturday 31 October 2015

'THEY CAN'T KEEP COMING BACK FROM GOING BEHIND,' THEY said.

'Tony Pulis teams are hard to beat,' they said.

'They will lose again at some point,' they said.

Leicester City respond on Halloween with a performance that would scare most teams in the Premier League. The story is still about Jamie Vardy, who scores in an eighth consecutive top flight game, and Riyad Mahrez, who nets twice to help turn this game in City's favour. More importantly, we're beginning to look like one of the best teams in the country.

We're on a high with our team flying at the top of the table and, in one sense, we won't get any higher than this all season. In fact, our travels have taken us from the docks at St Mary's a fortnight ago to The Hawthorns – the highest ground in England and Wales at just over 550 feet above sea level. Flags are pinned to the back of the away end in anticipation of what appears a winnable game.

There are key decisions which could go the way of the home side, especially when Robert Huth decides to rough up Albion's Gareth McAuley and Darren Fletcher inside the penalty area either side of half time, but the referee waves their appeals away.

Albion go ahead in predictable fashion through Salomon Rondon's near-post header from a corner. Yet City are impressive in open play, displaying more than enough verve and energy to give us hope. Vardy hits the inside of the post and the ball travels tantalisingly across the face of goal before it is cleared to safety.

We're arguably the better side in the first half but still manage to improve even more after the interval and quickly turn a one-goal deficit into a two-goal advantage. Mahrez grabs the first two, getting on the end of a pair of Marc Albrighton crosses from either flank and turning them both past Boaz Myhill in the Albion goal. The pundits didn't see this coming – the much-feted Pulis back line succumbing to two simple balls into the box. It's yet another comeback. They're losing the element of surprise.

The stand-out moment of the game arrives thirteen minutes from time with a goal typifying the season so far. Danny Drinkwater intercepts a pass outside his own penalty area and gives the ball to N'Golo Kanté. The Frenchman looks up and spots Vardy coming short to help retain possession. Kanté arrows the ball into Vardy, who turns it round the corner with one touch to the advancing Drinkwater. The home side's defence is being pulled all over the place. Drinkwater moves forward and measures a through ball for Vardy to run clear. There are three defenders in pursuit.

It's at this point, as Vardy collects the ball just inside the opposition half, that some City fans high in the away section at the other end of the ground prepare to celebrate. He still has nearly fifty yards to travel but his confidence could not be higher and Albion's notoriously slow defence are never going to catch him. Vardy's final touch before the shooting opportunity takes him slightly wide and Myhill comes out. The goalkeeper's optimism is misplaced. Vardy sweeps the ball into the far corner.

With beautiful symmetry, Vardy has scored with both feet at both ends of the same ground in the space of six months to mark an incredible period in the history of Leicester City Football Club. This game also ends 3-2 to the visitors, just as it did back in April, after Callum McManaman wins a dubious penalty and Rickie Lambert strikes the ball past Kasper Schmeichel.

The attacking interplay has been a joy to watch, reminiscent of one of the biggest clubs in the country going away from home and stamping their class all over a less illustrious opponent. That's not arrogance. It's just the way things feel at the moment, with a group of exceptionally talented footballers proving their worth above and beyond their price tags. Manchester City, Chelsea and Everton had all dismantled

West Bromwich Albion with three goals apiece this season before Ranieri and his squad arrived to do the same.

Importantly, Ranieri's decision to integrate Leonardo Ulloa into the starting line-up has not quelled City's threat on the break and the team manages to look vibrant while including a six-foot-three target man. If Ranieri can get the delicate balance right to blend height, pace, strength and creativity in his front four, the songs we sing on our way out of The Hawthorns might not just be a fantasy.

'Ranieri, Ranieri, Ranieri, he's taking us to Europe, to Europe, to Europe...'

West Bromwich Albion 2 (Rondon, Lambert)

Leicester City 3 (Mahrez 2, Vardy)

Team: Schmeichel, Simpson, Morgan, Huth, Schlupp, Albrighton (Dyer), Drinkwater (Okazaki), Kanté, Mahrez, Ulloa (King), Vardy

THE DOUBLE CROSSER

MARC ALBRIGHTON STANDS WITH HIS HANDS ON HIS HIPS, puffing his cheeks out. Four days earlier, he played the full 120 minutes in City's League Cup exit at Hull City's KC Stadium. Now, ten minutes into the second half of a real battle at The Hawthorns, Albrighton could be forgiven for being tired. Perhaps Claudio Ranieri is thinking of making a change.

Many of the current players have been said to embody the spirit of Leicester City Football Club – the commitment and desire of Jamie Vardy; the strength and resilience of Wes Morgan; the longevity and reliability of Andy King.

It wouldn't be the first time Marc Albrighton has been overlooked.

Albrighton provides the perfect combination of hard work and quality. Primary school marks, split equally between effort and achievement, spring to mind. You need both for success. Ranieri has also recognised the importance of balancing his midfield, with Riyad Mahrez's star turn on the right flank and the more defensively sound Albrighton on the left.

The young Albrighton appeared to be a one-trick pony, coming through the ranks at Aston Villa as a right winger who supplied cross after cross to a target man or goal poacher. Get it wide. He'd cross it in. Get it wide. He'd cross it in. He never really held down a regular place in the Villa team, but he grafted and he created chances for his strikers.

Aston Villa's management then made a decision as baffling as any that have led them to this season's relegation battle. In the summer of 2014, they released their hard-working, homegrown right winger.

Villa's loss was City's gain. Albrighton ticked so many boxes for the club's recruitment drive as they trawled lists of affordable players with Premier League experience. The move made sense to every party except Aston Villa.

Surprisingly, even as his new team struggled to gain results, Albrighton was overlooked. Fans were puzzled and, with no real explanation forthcoming, formed their own opinions about why. Perhaps he was poor in training. Perhaps he hadn't proved his fitness. Perhaps there was some kind of attitude problem.

It was a strange period, but Albrighton got his chance eventually in the right wing-back position when City moved to a 3-5-2 formation. It was the perfect fit and he played a key role in City's escape from relegation at the end of the 2014/15 season.

Ranieri's decision to switch back to 4-4-2 at the beginning of the following campaign posed a problem. How would he shoehorn Albrighton and Mahrez, both of whom thrive on the right wing, into the same line up? In fact, Albrighton slipped effortlessly into a new role on the left, often cutting inside to play through balls to Vardy or deliver high crosses to Mahrez at the far post.

That's what he does at The Hawthorns. The first cross comes from the left and floats high over the heads of City's strikers and West Bromwich Albion's defenders for the onrushing Mahrez to turn into the net. Minutes later, Albrighton sends a second cross in from the right. It takes a slight deflection and loops over everyone again to Mahrez, who puts City into the lead.

Comparisons to the much-loved team constructed by Martin O'Neill at the end of the last century can be tenuous, but Albrighton is reminiscent of O'Neill's trusty left winger Steve Guppy in the way he takes a touch to create half a yard of space before whipping a perfect cross into the box. He is consistent and reliable, qualities every bit as important in a successful side as Mahrez's ability to turn a game with magic. He seems a popular member of the dressing room and one with whom supporters can easily identify.

From the West Midlands to the East, from the right wing to the left, Marc Albrighton has found a new home in more ways than one.

12: WATFORD (H)

Saturday 7 November 2015

THERE WAS A TIME WHEN THE PROSPECT OF FACING WATFORD was unnerving. They were the cavaliers of the Championship, attacking at will and scoring goals for fun. Both clubs have been promoted since then but while the Hornets have steadily improved, City's transformation has been truly remarkable. It began before either had reached the top flight – an incredible turnaround that saw a devastating play-off semi-final defeat at Vicarage Road in May 2013 avenged with a masterful 3-0 victory less than six months later.

Even so, we could be forgiven for showing slight concern at the sight of Troy Deeney lining up against our side. It was Deeney's infamous breakaway goal that caused tears to be shed among the travelling support and fellow fans watching worldwide.

Part of City's progression has involved bringing in players who had previously never heard of the club, let alone considered it as a worthwhile career move. Riyad Mahrez said he thought we were a rugby club before he joined.

Sometimes it works the other way as well. Few of us had heard of N'Golo Kanté but, three months since putting pen to paper, Kanté has won over any doubters with a series of impressive displays at the heart of a vibrant midfield. He is a pocket dynamo and one of many players who epitomise what is happening at the club. He is exceptionally energetic, never gives up and, perhaps most startlingly of all, appears to be improving with every game.

Primarily, Kanté's game is to break up play and drive forward before feeding a more creative or destructive attacker. He will never be a scorer of many great goals, as demonstrated by his first for City – the goal that breaks Watford's resistance and sets the path for yet another victory.

Kanté shows good footwork to open up the hint of a sight of goal but his shot is weak and directed straight at Watford goalkeeper Heurelho Gomes. There was a time during his spell with Tottenham Hotspur when Gomes was a figure of fun in England for his unorthodox methods and the frequency of his mistakes. The Brazilian has recovered from those days to become a key performer for the newly-promoted Hornets but this is a flashback to his previous inconsistency. Gomes lets the ball trickle through his fingers and into the net.

It will be a struggle for Kanté to ever score a less impressive goal. Nevertheless, his first strike in English football gives the perfect opportunity to hail a new hero while more celebrated colleagues are having a quieter day.

Of course, Vardy still manages to score. We had thought the run and his season could be over when he fell in anguish during the second half. Instead, Vardy picks himself up and continues to motor around the field.

When Gomes brings him down inside the box, Mahrez is persuaded to hand the ball to his team-mate. Vardy smashes it in to make it nine consecutive games in which the England striker has scored in the Premier League.

Nine.

The record is ten.

Deeney gets on the scoresheet too with a penalty of his own after a foul by Kanté but the day belongs to City's goalscorers rather than the Watford man.

Last season, this type of game was a banana skin. There were so many occasions when a team outside of the elite turned up at the King Power Stadium and departed with at least a point. Goalless draws with Sunderland and Hull City and 1-0 defeats to West Bromwich Albion, Stoke City and Crystal Palace spring to mind. Watford certainly posed more of a challenge than most visitors this season and were unfortunate when a first-half Odion Ighalo shot came back off the post. This still had the feel of a routine home win and the campaign as a whole is beginning to seem like an entirely different beast to the long, hard slog of the previous one.

Not every game can be a swashbuckling end-to-end affair. Sometimes you just have to get through it and get the three points. This is already the seventh time in

12 games that City have achieved just that to rise to the dizzy heights of third in the Premier League table.

Leicester City 2 (Kanté, Vardy)

Watford 1 (Deeney)

Team: Schmeichel, Simpson, Morgan, Huth, Fuchs, Albrighton, Drinkwater (King), Kanté, Schlupp (Okazaki), Mahrez, Vardy

THE ANGLO-GERMAN ALLIANCE

AMONG THE BACK ROWS OF THE SOUTH-EAST CORNER OF THE home of Leicester City, a not-so-quiet revolution has taken place to mirror the transformation of the team's fortunes on the pitch. The singing is constant, often to the pounding beat of a drum, while flags and banners stretch out across the back of the South Stand depicting our heroes past and present – Claudio Ranieri is reimagined as The Godfather; Esteban Cambiasso is magic, you know. There are also flags bearing the name of the German club VfL Bochum.

This is SK1, home to the City fan group Union FS.

'For me and quite a few others, English football had lost its charm and incentive,' says James Challinor, one of the founders of the group. 'Prices were shooting up and Leicester's lack of direction around the time of the Sousa-Sven debacle suddenly meant spending time in Barnsley and Scunthorpe for a fifth consecutive year wasn't the most appealing way to spend your weekend – travelling into Europe and exploring other cities was.

'The irony was that we were swapping deprived, northern towns struggling for identity following the closure of their mines and steelworks for deprived German cities struggling to cope following the closure of their mines and steelworks.'

For almost ten years now, fans of Leicester City and VfL Bochum have been swapping scarves and stories of how their sides are the nearly men of their respective footballing nations: both poor in cup finals, both perennial yo-yo clubs, or 'Fahrstuhlmannschaften' – literally 'elevator club' in German, and both with limited experience in European competition.

'Fan friendships' like this are uncommon in Britain and largely alien to English fans. Without doubt the biggest on these shores is the relationship between fans of Ipswich Town and Fortuna Düsseldorf. Since 2006, Fortuna fans have been organising an annual trip to Suffolk, a recent example of which saw over 170 Germans taking their place in the Sir Bobby Robson Stand at Portman Road.

Ahead of City's home game with Watford, 29 Bochum fans, armed with Bochum-Leicester T-shirts and pin badges, waltzed into a Leicester city centre pub, confusing the locals on an otherwise non-descript Friday night in November. At the time, this was the largest delegation of supporters to travel in either direction.

Several Bochum supporters' groups were represented in the number that came to Leicester, including 'Blue-White Generation', or BWG, whose members include Julian Kruse, a fan who has helped to create a particularly strong bond with Union FS.

'Blue-White Generation is an old-school fan club, comparable to the thousands of Rangers or Celtic supporters' clubs all around the world,' says Kruse. 'In the late 1990s, fan clubs and hooligan groups were the most influential forces on the terraces. The members of BWG never had any interest in fighting, but just wanted to support Bochum home and away.'

BWG was founded in 1996 by the son of the former Bochum striker Helmut Kalinka, who originally played in the early 1930s for Germania Bochum – one of three clubs that contributed to the forming of VfL Bochum in 1938. The following year, Kalinka had to go to war. He was captured by the United States Army and was sent to America as a prisoner of war. While in captivity, he formed POW football teams to play against each other.

After he returned to Bochum in 1947, Kalinka continued to play for his home club and scored hundreds of goals. He retired in 1955 and stayed a club member until his death in 2015.

The dedication displayed by Kalinka and his son's continuation of that lifelong love for a football club seems far removed from the growing apathy felt by some City fans as Sven-Göran Eriksson splashed out on expensive misfits. It was the return to the true Leicester values of hard work and determination under his successor Nigel Pearson that saw the birth of Union FS.

'The concept came out of the way the 2013 season ended after Anthony Knock-aert's missed penalty at Watford,' says Challinor. 'A few of us felt the mood the following season could turn ugly, particularly after the way the club's form tailed off and then the lack of summer signings.'

Union FS was eventually founded by a collection of like-minded fans who wanted to improve the atmosphere at City's home ground in late December 2013. That initial meeting took place in a traditional pub called The Old Horse, opposite Victoria Park where the club, then known as Leicester Fosse, had played several matches in the 1880s.

Progress was initially slow with two or three trial games in the corner of SK1 marked out until the end of the 2013/14 season, the first of which saw a 3-0 victory over Charlton Athletic.

'We negotiated with the club and fans to designate an area in SK1 and managed to relocate a number of fans there to set up base from the start of our Premier League season,' says Challinor. 'Since then we have introduced flags, adding a more personal and unique feel to the Kop, which previously felt like any number of similar grounds. We also brought in a drum to help control the pace of songs.'

'Coming to home games is an entirely different proposition now,' says Jamie Treadwell, another founder member of the group. 'No more wondering if anyone will contribute to the atmosphere. No more concern that the team may or may not fight. No more questioning how we ended up in such a desperate place.'

'In this modern football, 'everything-is-evil' era that we are living in, it almost feels like we have taken football back to its roots. Singing for 90 minutes, bouncing around and having a laugh with your mates. Giving everything for the cause and just generally enjoying yourself. The way it's meant to be. And it's infectious. It's spreading. More and more people across the Kop are getting involved all the time, buying into it and wanting to be a part of it.'

Union FS have added noise and colour to City's home games but they have also brought the cult of the tifo: an irregular series of fan-funded, continental-type displays that take up the whole of the Kop.

'I'm convinced the first tifo of this season in the opening game against Sunderland had a positive influence and set the tone for the season,' says Challinor.

The tifo depicted two supporters, one holding a scarf aloft and another waving a flag. A prophetic message along the bottom of the display read: 'Your colours are in our hands, our dreams are in yours', the latter part of which has been a mantra repeated throughout the season by Claudio Ranieri. The fans are allowed to dream. The players must instead work and fight.

There is clearly a heavy European influence on the mentality of Union FS and Julian Kruse believes Ranieri's messages, underlining the importance of hard graft, strike a chord with fans of his own club.

'Bochum is a multi-cultural city with a typical working class attitude,' says Kruse. 'This determines how we love our football: you can't win every game, but the players must fight and never give up. Bochum is stuck between two of the biggest clubs in Germany – Schalke 04 and Borussia Dortmund – so we always have been and will be the 'underdog', staying in the shadows of these two title-winning teams.

'As bigger numbers of Bochum fans started to travel to Leicester, the friendship got noticed by more and more Leicester fans outside Union FS,' he says. 'The people in England were very interested why on earth we would support, in their words, such a boring, mediocre club from the Midlands who can't win anything important.'

'Once we told them that the whole friendship is not about winning titles but supporting a 'twin club', we received a lot of respect and friendliness. There has been not a single Leicester fan who has walked up to me and said that he or she doesn't like us or the friendship between the two sets of supporters.

'After all, Leicester and Bochum have lots of things in common,' says Kruse. 'The city of Leicester developed in a similar way to Bochum concerning industry and immigration and the people can be a little bit rough sometimes but open-minded and friendly at the same time.

'Talking about football, the rivalry between Leicester City, Nottingham Forest and Derby County reminds me of the typical Ruhr area football agenda – your team always comes first, even if it's less successful. Nowadays, both Leicester and Bochum are 'the club without rivals'.'

But with friends like these, who cares about enemies anyway?

13: NEWCASTLE UNITED (A)

Saturday 21 November 2015

ON FRIDAY 13 NOVEMBER 2015, TERRORISTS COMMIT A SERIES OF atrocities in the city of Paris. 130 people are killed and hundreds injured. One of the targets is the Stade de France, where the French national side are playing a friendly against Germany. The perpetrators are prevented from entering the stadium, an act which surely saves hundreds of lives. As the world comes to terms with the tragedy, in particular the horror endured that night by those inside music venue Le Bataclan, thoughts inevitably turn to the safety of future major sporting events. Leicester City players and supporters will attend the 2016 European Championships in cities across France. Within days of the attacks in Paris, there are further international matches postponed in Belgium and Germany due to the threat of terrorism.

Two of City's star performers, Riyad Mahrez and N'Golo Kanté, were born in the French capital. While Mahrez chose to play international football for Algeria, there has understandably been talk of Kanté being close to a call-up to the France squad. He would have wanted to be on the pitch at the Stade de France that night.

The Premier League announces that the French national anthem will be played before each of the weekend's fixtures.

This is the sombre backdrop to Leicester City's long trip to the north east, over-shadowing the main footballing story which remains Jamie Vardy's attempt to set a new record for scoring in consecutive Premier League games. City's visit to St James' Park represents game ten in Vardy's run and the chance to equal Ruud Van Nistelrooy's current record, set on the same ground in 2003.

It happens in first half stoppage time and it's a fittingly great goal. Vardy plays a one-two with his strike partner Leonardo Ulloa before turning Moussa Sissoko, firing in at the near post and running to celebrate in the corner beneath the travelling support. His team-mates are ecstatic at his achievement, something that says a lot about the side's team spirit. Wes Morgan runs to Vardy and lifts him high into the air. Even the home fans offer a polite round of applause in recognition.

City add two more goals in the second half as the Magpies disintegrate. Ulloa is left unmarked at the back post to head in a Mahrez cross and substitute Shinji Okazaki scrambles in a scrappy third. It's also just the second clean sheet of the season.

People are beginning to question whether this Leicester City team is better than the one assembled by Martin O'Neill in the late 1990s. O'Neill's side did the business over the space of four years, not six months, but there were few occasions when they dominated away from home playing free-flowing, attacking football. The most goals any of O'Neill's players scored in a single Premier League season was Tony Cottee's total of thirteen in the 1999/2000 season, another record Vardy equals with his latest strike.

Despite our long stay at the foot of the table last season, the King Power never looked like St James' Park does when Mike Jones blows the final whistle. Half empty. Boos ringing out. Newcastle aren't even in the bottom three and have cobbled together a points tally of ten.

In contrast, Mahrez and Kanté both have huge smiles on their faces as do thousands of City fans packed into the uppermost of upper tiers in Newcastle because Leicester City have just gone top of the Premier League.

And this isn't a couple of games in. This isn't a heady afternoon of August heat. There is snow at the side of the pitch and the final whistle is greeted by the dull thud of applause created by gloved hands. It's freezing. It's nearly December. And we're top.

The media tell us it will only last a couple of hours because Manchester City are playing in the evening kick-off and a victory would send them to the summit. Yet they lose 4-1 at home to Liverpool and fail to take top spot. The two Manchester clubs take up second and third position, hotly pursued by the two north London sides in fourth and fifth.

On the long trip home, we cheer the result from the Etihad Stadium knowing our team will remain top of the league for at least seven days and the visit of Manchester United in November's final fixture will be a televised clash between first place and second.

Newcastle United 0

Leicester City 3 (Vardy, Ulloa, Okazaki)

Team: Schmeichel, Simpson, Morgan, Huth, Fuchs, Mahrez (Dyer), Drinkwater, Kanté, Albrighton, Ulloa (Okazaki), Vardy (King)

THE CONDUCTOR

DANNY DRINKWATER WAS SIGNED FROM MANCHESTER UNITED in January 2012. He began the 2013/14 season cupping his ears to the travelling Leicester City fans after scoring the club's first goal of the campaign. He ended it with a Championship winner's medal, having been voted the Player of the Year by City supporters. At the end-of-season awards, Nigel Pearson described Drinkwater as a 'complex character', a vague insight into the relationship between our imposing manager and midfield playmaker.

That description caused intrigue among supporters. What exactly did Pearson mean? It is so rare that a player is described in anything other than overwhelmingly glowing terms by their manager, especially when their efforts have just been recognised by the fans.

Interviews with Drinkwater were rare. We wondered what made him tick. Later that summer, he said something that all supporters want to hear from one of their best players: 'I am more than happy to stay here for the rest of my career if that is what the club wants.'

There it was, set in stone: Danny Drinkwater was looking forward to his first full season in the Premier League and beyond.

One year on, Claudio Ranieri reflected on Drinkwater's involvement over the previous twelve months and decided that he had been underused. The addition of N'Golo Kanté to the City midfield meant Drinkwater's workload would be reduced slightly and we soon saw a vastly improved player who, even at the top level, began to resemble his own hero, Paul Scholes, in his calmness in possession and accurate long passing.

Danny Drinkwater stepped into a new role as the conductor of Ranieri's orchestra. He started to dictate the tempo and co-ordinate all around him into a single, cohesive unit. Ranieri decided his team played better without the ball so Drinkwater was not playing the same role as most midfielders charged with controlling games. Ranieri wanted him to control midfield even when we didn't have possession.

Drinkwater's range of passing is immaculate but he sacrificed that for the team and used it to benefit his colleagues. The long pass from Drinkwater to Jamie Vardy became a template for success, utilising both players' strengths to maximum effect.

It had been tough on Danny Drinkwater, a lifelong Manchester United supporter, to leave Old Trafford. He has no regrets now.

14: MANCHESTER UNITED (H)

Saturday 28 November 2015

AHEAD OF THE VISIT OF MANCHESTER UNITED, JAMIE VARDY has 13 goals in 13 games. In his first 26 appearances last season, he scored just once. But what a goal it was.

September 2014. The score is Leicester City 3 Manchester United 3. Juan Mata has the ball ten yards inside the City half. In just four touches, it will be in the back of United's net.

One: Ritchie De Laet robs Mata and charges upfield. United, who have been pouring forward in search of a winner, have left Vardy one-on-one with rookie defender Tyler Blackett. The youngster leaves his man to engage De Laet.

Two: De Laet threads the ball through to Vardy. So much space. A second or two to savour the moment. We rise in anticipation.

Three: Vardy controls the bouncing ball with his midriff, directing it in front of him. Blackett can't recover. Chris Smalling can't recover. Wayne Rooney has sprinted back in a vain attempt to make a tackle. He's not getting anywhere close. Just the goalkeeper to beat: David De Gea - the best goalkeeper in the Premier League. This is the chance to put City into a 4-3 lead against Manchester United. We had been

3-1 down. Vardy opens up his body and prepares to strike.

Four: Vardy calmly strokes the ball past De Gea into the corner of the net. Just nonchalantly side-footed as though this isn't the most pressurised moment of his entire football career.

Scenes, as the kids say. Absolute scenes.

And then, nothing. For another 23 games. It's difficult to know what is more improbable – the coolness of Vardy's finish past De Gea that day in September, the fact he didn't score again until 21 March of the following year or his 100% goals-to-games ratio so far this season.

That's all in the past though. Now Manchester United are back at the King Power and the focus on Jamie Vardy is even more intense in the build-up to this game than when he was running towards De Gea about to score his first ever Premier League goal. Vardy has scored in ten consecutive games to equal the record set by former United legend Ruud Van Nistelrooy, meaning he can break it against Louis Van Gaal's side.

In fact, the spotlight shines brightly on the entire club in the run-up to a game which will be televised live on Sky Sports. It's first against second and everybody is talking about the team at the top. Vardy is hogging the headlines but there are also plenty of column inches devoted to the likes of Claudio Ranieri, Riyad Mahrez, Danny Drinkwater and N'Golo Kanté.

So here it is. Leicester City versus Manchester United – take two.

It's cold. It's dark. It's windy. It's wet. Before kick-off, a tifo display at the Kop end includes illustrations of three City heroes: Vardy, Mahrez and Schlupp.

Really, it's all about Vardy tonight and everything is building towards one moment. That moment comes halfway through the first half. Kasper Schmeichel claims a United corner inside his six-yard box and finds Christian Fuchs with a quick throw. United's inexperienced centre-back Paddy McNair is more concerned with getting back into his defensive half than monitoring Fuchs and so the Austrian moves off McNair to an unfamiliar right-sided position. Fuchs carries the ball unopposed over the halfway line until he is level with the edge of the centre circle inside United's half. He switches back onto his favoured left foot and spots a familiar run from a City attacker.

It goes without saying. It's Jamie Vardy. United have left two defenders back to cover the counter attack: Matteo Darmian and Ashley Young. Darmian is on the near side and looks best placed to deal with the danger. Young finds himself on the far side and caught between two plans – unable to play Vardy offside and certainly not quick enough to cope with his opponent's acceleration. Vardy points where he wants the ball to go and is thankful that it will be delivered by Fuchs. It looks momentarily as though Darmian can cut it out but, perhaps wary of conceding a penalty, he lets it run by.

The ball reaches Vardy and his first touch takes him across Darmian and in on goal. For the second time in just over a year, Jamie Vardy is faced with David De Gea. The angle is tight and De Gea has to shift over to his left. This is where we see Vardy's confidence come into the equation. He knows he is running wide and hasn't got time to take a glance at the goalkeeper. He knows he has to hit it. Of course, he knows exactly where the goal is as well. The crowd rises. De Gea's body position leaves space for a shot into the far corner. A trademark Vardy strike of the ball, launching himself into the air with the cleanest of contact.

It's in.

Vardy heads off towards L1, one of the two noisiest sections in the ground. He's yelling at the United fans, at the City fans, at the cameras, at his team-mates.

'All mine!'

And it is. The record is his. Jamie Vardy has scored in eleven consecutive Premier League games, beating the record set by Manchester United's own Ruud Van Nistelrooy in 2003.

Complete pandemonium all around the King Power Stadium. This is some moment. Not just a Leicester City goal. Not just a Leicester City goal against Manchester United. A historic moment in football terms. It's two celebrations rolled into one. One for the team. One for the player. The noise is deafening. The score is 1-0.

Unfortunately, it doesn't end that way. Bastian Schweinsteiger pulls United level in first half stoppage time with a header from close range after City fail to defend a routine corner. An atmosphere that had been building to fever pitch falls strangely flat as the players head to the dressing rooms.

The second half is played out with increasing dullness. United retain possession at all costs. City fall back towards Schmeichel's goal but there is only one good opportunity at either end. From another corner, Schweinsteiger is denied by a Schmeichel save. The best chance is created when Riyad Mahrez dribbles half the length of the pitch and feeds a through ball to substitute Leonardo Ulloa. The Argentine cuts onto his right foot and shoots weakly straight at De Gea when a firm shot either side of the goalkeeper would have given City a precious lead.

The game fizzles out, quite at odds with the outpouring of emotion after Vardy's landmark goal. Manchester City's victory over Southampton earlier in the afternoon means they end the weekend top of the table and Arsenal's failure to win at Carrow Road keeps the Gunners in fourth. City have played another of the big boys and this time they have avoided defeat, meaning they enter December in second place, only kept off top spot on goal difference.

Leicester City 1 (Vardy)
Manchester United 1 (Schweinsteiger)
Team: Schmeichel, Simpson (De Laet), Morgan, Huth, Fuchs, Mahrez, Drinkwater, Kanté, Albrighton (Schlupp), Okazaki (Ulloa), Vardy

THE PHENOMENON

JAMIE VARDY HAS BECOME A PHENOMENON. IT'S A FAIRY TALE within a fairy tale and Vardy leads from the front with ferocious work rate and a determination to upset the odds.

Before the great escape began in April 2015, we were the only football fans interested in Jamie Vardy. Now everybody's talking about him. He strikes fear into every defender in the Premier League.

Vardy's story seems to have been covered by every media outlet in the world. They all write about his release from his boyhood club, Sheffield Wednesday, his first-team grounding with Stocksbridge Park Steels in the seventh tier of English football, his modest wages and his job in a carbon fibre factory. They write about his assault conviction, the tag he had to wear and the curfew he had to observe. They write about his move to Halifax, then to Fleetwood and finally to Nigel Pearson's Leicester in the summer of 2012 for a non-league record £1million.

This is where City fans can take up the story, because the leap from Vardy's Hillsborough exit to his arrival at the King Power seemed extraordinary but he took two equally large strides after that. The first – adjusting to higher levels and retaining belief in his ability – took three years and resulted in an England call-up. The second – breaking a Premier League goalscoring record – took three months and established Vardy as a global sensation.

As with most signings, it all began for City supporters with a YouTube video. There have been plenty over the years: six different angles of an Iranian right-back performing a karate kick on Cristiano Ronaldo; a collection of wonder goals by a French second division forward who, it has to be said, looked decent but ultimately broke our hearts; a Ghanaian centre-back controlling an opposition long ball in injury time and sprinting the length of the pitch to win a penalty.

Like Hossein Kaebi, Yann Kermorgant and Daniel Amartey, we were impressed with what we saw of Vardy. His highlights at Conference level showcased the breakneck pace and accurate finishing that have graced the Premier League this season. He appeared to play mainly from the left, cutting inside to hare past leaden-footed non-league defenders before slotting the ball calmly into the far corner of the net.

The player we witnessed in that first Championship season displayed glimpses of these qualities, but his first touch so often let him down and his confidence appeared to drop as the scale of the challenge dawned. This was a huge step up.

A year on from his big move, Vardy believed he wasn't good enough. In a scene that Hollywood scriptwriters must already have pencilled into their plans, his manager Nigel Pearson convinced him otherwise and a place in the starting line-up for the opening day trip to Middlesbrough was his.

We knew nothing then of Vardy's heart-to-heart with Pearson, nor could we have foreseen his subsequent upturn in form. A winning goal at the Riverside Stadium was the catalyst for a remarkable season for both player and club. City became champions, with Vardy a key figure. His first touch was vastly improved and he looked like a finisher again, scoring key goals on tricky Tuesday night trips to Barnsley and Birmingham. Those are the kind of wins that teams need to escape the Championship, usually while the rest of the footballing world is focused on Champions League games taking place on the same evening. It's hard work, and Vardy was exactly the right man for the job.

There was much anticipation about Vardy's introduction to the Premier League. Having honed his technique and concentrated on his strengths, it was time to use his pace and take some expensively assembled back lines by surprise.

There were ups and downs during his first season in the top flight. The highlights sandwiched a lengthy period when Vardy again looked short of the required standard. His initial impact came with a Man of the Match display in the 5-3 win over Manchester United in September. His most telling contributions were winning goals against West Bromwich Albion and Burnley in April to help secure the club's survival. Leonardo Ulloa was the top goalscorer that season and Vardy often played a supporting role, most commonly to be found running the channels instead of directly threatening opposition centre-backs. Vardy's efforts during City's great escape showed him to be capable of leading the line for City at Premier League level.

The summer threw up another curveball with the sacking of the man who had placed so much faith in Vardy. Would Claudio Ranieri keep that faith or would he enter the transfer market to seek a replacement? The omens appeared good. A first England call-up provided a confidence boost. City's first pre-season game at Lincoln saw Ranieri introduce Vardy at half-time and clearly enjoy the immediate injection of pace and energy to the team's front line.

The obvious move would have been to sign a goalscorer to play alongside Vardy. Instead, City signed Shinji Okazaki, one of the few strikers in European football who could match his fitness and commitment, and therefore lightened the load on the number nine. Okazaki ran the channels. Vardy stayed on the shoulder of the last man and waited for a through ball.

It was a recipe for success, but those who concentrated on Vardy's fascinating back story or even his record-breaking goalscoring run managed to miss something equally impressive. Jamie Vardy had become one of the best footballers in the country. There has been so much said about his pace, work rate and ability to stretch defences that his technical improvement has been taken for granted, but this is a player whose first touch was often found wanting at Championship level.

Even two-thirds of the way through the 2014/15 season, it seemed unthinkable that Vardy could lead the line for a top flight City side. His turnaround is every bit as remarkable as the Leicester City story itself, summed up by a moment in the 2-1 win at Carrow Road that would have passed many people by entirely.

The ball is played up to Vardy on the halfway line with his back to goal. At The Hawthorns some weeks later, he will find himself in this situation and play a quick one-two with Danny Drinkwater before racing clear to put City 3-1 up. But there is no support right now, so Vardy's first touch is excellent, he uses his strength to hold off his marker and he takes the ball out to the flanks before laying it off to a team-mate. This example of intelligence and assuredness is a snapshot of a vastly improved footballer.

Of course, the work rate is still there. Vardy's commitment to the cause has never been questioned and now acts as a perfect reference point for any player joining the club. Everybody is expected to work. Vardy is a shining example of the benefits for both the individual and the collective.

We've always loved a hard worker. Now our hard worker just happens to be feared throughout the Premier League.

15: SWANSEA CITY (A)

Saturday 5 December 2015

GO WEST, AS THE PET SHOP BOYS ONCE SANG. AND KEEP going west until the view to your left is a post-apocalyptic cityscape of metal constructions billowing white into the sky. It looks like a scene from a science fiction film. It's actually just Port Talbot Steel Works and you're on your way to Swansea.

Two hours before kick-off, hundreds of Leicester City fans disembark coaches straight into a howling gale. The wind will have died down by the time we return but we will still be staggering around, dazed by another afternoon that feels more like fantasy than science fiction. Has there ever been a more surreal season in the club's history?

There is also disbelief that Jamie Vardy has completed a league game without scoring for the first time since a sweltering day in August. Thankfully, despite what some have been saying, City are not a one-man team. If Vardy doesn't get you then Riyad Mahrez will.

Ranieri makes one change with Leonardo Ulloa returning in place of Shinji Okazaki, signalling his preference for the Argentine's greater attacking threat against weaker sides. Ulloa's inclusion also demonstrates Ranieri's unswerving confidence in his team's work ethic, fitness and growing defensive resilience. City are one of very few Premier League teams to consistently play 4-4-2 in an era of lone strikers and packed midfields.

The plan works perfectly. Swansea's style of play, a blend of laborious passing patterns and lack of movement off the ball, is ripe for the plucking. N'Golo Kanté has a field day, repeatedly stealing the ball and dribbling unopposed. There are five clear chances before the break and Mahrez takes two of them, deflecting a corner in at the near post after just five minutes and then finishing after good work from Kanté halfway through the first half. Vardy wastes a clear one-on-one with Swans goalkeeper Lukasz Fabianski, Ulloa shoots just past the post following another counter attack and Mahrez puts a shot straight at Fabianski with both strikers well placed for a telling pass.

Garry Monk stands on the edge of his technical area barking instructions but nobody's listening. The City fans sing that Monk will be sacked in the morning. It will be a few days longer but the end result is the same. Monk is dismissed in midweek. Swansea hit the post and bar in search of a way back into the game during the second half but the third goal is scored at the other end when another Kanté raid ends with Vardy setting up Mahrez for a simple finish. Irresistible football from a team that is quickly becoming an irresistible force.

Manchester City's surprise defeat at Stoke in the lunchtime kick-off means that Ranieri's men return to the top of the Premier League. Jamie Vardy's record run has come to an end and the media focus switches to the collective rather than the individual. Kanté's eye-catching involvement in two of the three goals at Swansea is featured on Match of the Day. It's nice to see an unsung hero receive recognition for his work but we'd prefer it if nobody noticed one of the best footballers in Europe playing in our central midfield each week. He's ours. Hands off.

Mahrez's hat-trick is the first of his career after scoring twice against both Sunderland and West Bromwich Albion already this season. He moves into double figures for the season and only Vardy has scored more Premier League goals. Mahrez's finishing proved erratic prior to Ranieri's arrival at the club but his game has certainly developed under the Italian. He has been given greater licence to roam down the right wing to find space behind the full-back.

Mahrez has also thrived in the lack of respect afforded to his talent by successive opposition managers. Over and over at Swansea, both full-backs pushed forward in a way they seemed unlikely to replicate against traditionally big clubs. Yet Mahrez and Vardy have demonstrated this season that they are among the league's elite performers and deserve special plans designed to prevent them wreaking havoc. As the quality of teams City will face improves during the winter period, it will be interesting to see how the opposition plan to shut down the likes of Mahrez on the counter.

The coaches arrive back in Leicester twelve hours after their morning departure. It's a long day but it's worth it. We have travelled around 750 miles in total to our past two away games. In the corresponding fixtures last season, we saw our team concede three and score none. This time around City have hit six without reply. The amazing turnaround continues and will certainly be driven home by our next fixture: the champions are coming to town with a seventeen-point deficit to make up.

Swansea City 0
Leicester City 3 (Mahrez 3)
Team: Schmeichel, Simpson, Morgan, Huth, Fuchs, Mahrez (Schlupp), Drinkwater, Kanté, Albrighton, Ulloa (King), Vardy

THE RASH

THE CROWNING GLORY OF CITY'S IMPRESSIVE SUMMER recruitment was the signing of French central midfielder N'Golo Kanté – one of the finest footballers ever to wear the blue shirt.

To truly understand Kanté's importance, we need to go back in time to the late 1990s.

The lynchpin of Martin O'Neill's successful Leicester City side was Neil Lennon, a defensive midfielder from Lurgan in Northern Ireland. Lennon was not especially quick, nor was he tall or even very strong, but the entire team was built around his reassuring presence. He would sit in front of the defence, win the ball and pass it. He didn't score many goals and he never won that many plaudits outside of Leicestershire and his home country. He was brilliant though, and City's failure to replace him when he moved to Celtic in October 2000 was a major factor in the club's subsequent decline.

Even by the 2014/15 season, City had never truly replaced Neil Lennon. Successive managers had failed to find a player with the quality to run a game at the highest level. Esteban Cambiasso brought leadership and experience to City's struggle to survive in the Premier League but, approaching 35 years of age, he could never be a long-term answer and his exit meant another mission to find a player who could dominate midfield against the most illustrious opponents.

Steve Walsh and his scouting team had identified precisely the right man for the job: N'Golo Kanté – a 24-year-old French-Malian from Caen in Ligue 1. Kanté's name appeared in the media early in the summer but the exit of Nigel Pearson and rival interest from Marseille meant the trail went cold for some weeks. It appeared that City had moved on to other targets – OGC Nice's Nampalys Mendy and Nantes midfielder Jordan Veretout seemed to be on the radar along with several other names – but it would later be revealed that Walsh was desperate to secure Kanté's signature. When Claudio Ranieri took over as manager, Walsh lobbied him daily to bring Kanté to the club.

At this point, City were desperate for central midfielders. One of the longest-running sagas of a summer jam-packed with neverending stories was the reported pursuit of Internacional's Chilean international Charles Aranguiz. City fans were intrigued. Aranguiz looked such an accomplished player that the chances of him signing for a club that had just escaped relegation to the Championship must have been slim.

A shady tale ensued involving a mysterious representative named Anderson Perry and the 'steering wheel', Google's translation for Aranguiz's pivote position at the base of midfield. This was truly crazy stuff, the kind of transfer window madness that makes anything that happens on a football pitch – even the most improbable events or results – look positively normal, but that's what you get when you cross poorly translated reports from South America with messageboards full of supporters desperate for information.

Aranguiz went to Bayer Leverkusen. Veretout went to Aston Villa. Mendy went nowhere. But what about Kanté?

Thankfully, Walsh got his man. Kanté signed for City and prepared to make the transition from the French top flight to the Premier League.

Of course, City also signed the Swiss international captain Gökhan Inler which meant Kanté had plenty of competition for his place. The season began with the two central midfield positions taken by two long-standing players, Andy King and Danny Drinkwater, with Kanté on the substitutes bench and Inler soon to join him.

Inler had pedigree. Kanté was unknown. Yet when Ranieri introduced the pair, one shone and the other struggled to adapt. Kanté was a revelation. City supporters looked at each other in amazement. What a player.

Immediately, Kanté was tackling and intercepting more than any player we could remember. Drinkwater nicknamed him 'The Rash'. He was all over his opponents. His anticipation was unrivalled, his tackling was precise and he ran all day as though powered by electricity. Kanté's movement was constant, seeking out the ball and winning it cleanly before giving it to a team-mate. He was quick too.

After a few weeks, he started keeping the ball after winning it and bursting through midfield at speed. Riyad Mahrez owed his hat-trick goal at Swansea to a driving Kanté run past several helpless defenders. Kanté even started winning headers, leaping high into the air above much taller opponents. At Newcastle, Mahrez was able to cross for Leonardo Ulloa to score City's second goal because Kanté launched himself into an unlikely header in midfield.

Now he isn't just stopping the opposition playing. He contributes to City attacks as well. It often feels like there are two Kantés out there, or three. Time and time again, City fans have the same conversation – even when Schmeichel has made save after save, Morgan has been at his imposing best and Vardy or Mahrez have scored the winner.

'Man of the match today?'

'Probably N'Golo.'

Kanté's first goal for the club came against Watford, a toe poke which squirmed through the gloves of Heurelho Gomes and trickled into the net. He celebrated the same way he does when his team-mates score – a wide grin and a modest round of applause. A model professional, then, who always works hard for his team-mates and is too shy to take centre stage, but also – even just a few months into his Leicester City career – one of the greatest players ever to wear the shirt. That's the amazing thing about N'Golo Kanté: surrounded by players having the season of their lives, he is the best of all.

Finally, Leicester City have replaced Neil Lennon – the most important piece of the jigsaw has fallen perfectly into place.

16: CHELSEA (H)

Monday 14 December 2015

LET'S GET ONE THING STRAIGHT. THIS IS THE MOST SURREAL period in the history of Leicester City Football Club. It is also one of the biggest transformations the English top flight has ever seen. In the Premier League era, it is clearly unparalleled.

In fact, it's almost as though the tongue-in-cheek terrace chant has come true and Leicester City are Chelsea in disguise. Christmas is still two weeks away and the reigning league champions are already coming to terms with the inevitability of losing their title.

After Chelsea's previous visit to the King Power Stadium, a 3-1 victory that enabled them to place one hand on the Premier League trophy, José Mourinho's men were 49 points ahead of City in the table. Both teams have played nineteen league games since that night and City go into the corresponding fixture 17 points clear of our opponents.

Pre-season predictions and previews marked Chelsea out as clear favourites to retain their title with ease. The fall from grace in the past four months has been spectacular. There were approving cheers as the City fans' coaches and cars skirted the south of Birmingham following victory over Swansea. Newly-promoted AFC Bournemouth had just beaten Chelsea at Stamford Bridge.

That was Chelsea's eighth league defeat of a startlingly poor campaign so far, meaning they arrive at the King Power Stadium just one point above the relegation zone. Nobody knows quite what to expect. It has been a season of surprises throughout the league. What would be more of a shock though? City maintaining a fine start with victory over the champions? Or Chelsea ensuring their hosts lose in the league for only the second time since their previous visit?

Bookmakers favour Chelsea in spite of current form. They still possess proven quality throughout their team and most neutrals are waiting for City's bubble to burst. The game will be televised live on Monday night following another weekend of shock results across the Premier League. While Arsenal and Manchester City both won to move into first and second place respectively, there were defeats for Manchester United and Tottenham Hotspur. Liverpool and Everton could both only manage draws. Can Leicester City return to top spot?

The answer is emphatic, delivered by one of the greatest teams the club has ever fielded. A bold statement but this is once-in-a-lifetime stuff. The champions of England, managed by a multiple European Cup winner, are humbled at the King Power. When the final whistle blows, they lie twenty points behind City. It feels like a defining match in many ways – a win that Claudio Ranieri will maintain just brings City closer to the goal of survival but the subtext is clear. The media, neutrals and even some fans doubted the credentials of these players. It gets harder to do so with every passing performance.

Understandably, the team is unchanged – Schmeichel, Simpson, Morgan, Huth, Fuchs, Mahrez, Kanté, Drinkwater, Albrighton, Ulloa, Vardy. Even when Danny Drinkwater is forced off by a hamstring injury early in the game, Andy King slots in seamlessly. On the contrary, Chelsea have star names but can't match City in any department. Kasper Schmeichel is a virtual bystander during a first half dominated, in terms of attacking intent rather than possession, by the home side.

The opening goal comes just after the half hour mark and it's a belter. N'Golo Kanté plays a sharp pass to the feet of Jamie Vardy, who turns it round the corner to Leonardo Ulloa. Chelsea full-back Cesar Azpilicueta is drawn to the Argentine and leaves Riyad Mahrez free on the right hand side. In his current form, Mahrez only needs a bit of space to wreak havoc.

Earlier in the season, he might have opted to take on Azpilicueta, twisting and turning on his way into the box. There is a notable difference in Mahrez's play at present though and instead he delivers an early ball towards the six yard box. John

Terry can't cut it out and Vardy nips ahead of his marker Kurt Zouma to hit a volley. The ball flies past Thibaut Courtois in the Chelsea goal and Vardy completes a similar curving run of celebration to the one he made after scoring in the same net against Manchester United a fortnight earlier.

There are two things that elevate the goal to greatness: firstly, the two protagonists could hardly have been given a higher profile before the game and José Mourinho was still unable to prevent their lethal combination; secondly, there was no need to rely on the counter attack that has brought City so many goals this season – instead, they simply carved straight through the massed ranks of their heralded opposition.

Mahrez's goal to double City's tally is every bit as good as Vardy's opener. It's individual brilliance rather than a deadly link-up, despite good work from King and Albrighton in the approach. Azpilicueta again leaves Mahrez free, this time at the back post as a high ball from Albrighton sails over. Mahrez brings it under his spell with one touch, feints and dummies Azpilicueta once, twice, then a third time to work half a yard of space before sending a curling effort beyond the considerable reach of Courtois into the far corner. There's something about the ball hitting the net that feels like a moment, a crescendo, like a beat dropping at a festival. A momentary sense of anticipation and then bang: a brilliant goal, all the more satisfying given its context.

Inevitably, pressure comes from Mourinho's team and Chelsea substitute Loic Remy eventually pulls a goal back with a close range header following good work down the left from fellow replacement Pedro Rodriguez. All four stands produce a wall of noise during the closing minutes as Ranieri's increasingly tired troops drop towards Schmeichel's goal.

City have earned a tag as comeback kings this season but the ability of these players to close out a game has flown under the radar a little. Count the teams who have failed to equalise despite late pressure: West Bromwich Albion, Crystal Palace, Watford, West Ham United, Norwich City and now Chelsea. That's effectively twelve points earned through impressive rearguard actions and City cling on for another maximum haul.

The celebrations are long and loud and continue in homes and offices throughout the county for another week in which City will remain top of the Premier League. The champions can only look on in envy.

Leicester City 2 (Vardy, Mahrez)

Chelsea 1 (Remy)

Team: Schmeichel, Simpson, Morgan, Huth, Fuchs, Mahrez (Inler), Drinkwater (King), Kanté, Albrighton, Ulloa, Vardy (Okazaki)

THE HOKEY-COKEY

WHEN TRYING TO EXPLAIN WHAT IS HAPPENING AT LEICESTER City Football Club this season, the character of the players is a good starting point. The likes of Kasper Schmeichel, Wes Morgan and Jamie Vardy are clearly committed to achieving great things for the club at any cost, putting their bodies on the line to ensure the team keeps winning.

Look past the first names on the teamsheet and even those waiting in reserve are men of incredible character. City will need to call on two of them for the last game before Christmas: Andy King, already a legend at the age of 27 after years of service in the Football League, and Marcin Wasilewski, who became a hero almost as soon as he pulled on the blue shirt.

Like so many of his team-mates, Wasilewski has a great story to accompany his place in a squad surpassing all expectations. On 30 August 2009, he suffered a horrific broken leg when playing for Anderlecht against fierce rivals Standard Liege and missed almost the entire season.

'I am a hard worker,' said Wasilewski after his recovery from injury. 'I am not afraid of the sacrifices that lie ahead. I know I have been given a second footballing life and I want to make the most of it.'

'Wasyl' joined City three years later and we soon experienced the spirit that endeared him to Anderlecht fans and the bond that had formed between them. We saw it first hand at one Championship game against Millwall when a group of enthusiastic Belgians took over a quiet corner of the King Power and sang in support of their Polish hero. Brilliant photographs later surfaced online showing Wasyl being mobbed by Anderlecht fans on the touchline next to the West Stand long after the final whistle.

Although he was a key figure alongside captain Wes Morgan as City won promotion to the Premier League, many fans felt the top flight would be too quick for a player who had just turned 34. Not for the first time, Wasyl showed his doubters who was boss by performing admirably in difficult circumstances. City struggled until the miraculous turnaround in April but Wasilewski had a fine season throughout.

The form of Morgan and Robert Huth this season has meant very limited opportunities for City's popular Pole but despite Huth's suspension for the trip to Everton, the Toffees attackers would know to prepare for a battle.

17: EVERTON (A)

Saturday 19 December 2015

IN THE THOMAS FROST, A PUB A FEW HUNDRED YARDS FROM Goodison Park, a tinny speaker is blasting out Everton chants at ear-splitting volume. We escape into the swirling rain. A woman hands out free mince pies that taste of petrol. Fake snow is blown across the path.

This is top flight football in 2015 but it could be a scene from thirty years ago, when Leicester City were the visitors for the Toffees' last home game before Christmas on 14 December 1985. On our way into the ground, we reflect that we haven't won in the league at Everton since that day's unlikely 2-1 victory.

A huge image of Howard Kendall clutching the 1985 First Division trophy looks down from the side of the Goodison Road stand. Thirty years on, we're the title challengers. Leicester City are aiming for a third successive win to stay top of the Premier League at Christmas.

Claudio Ranieri makes three changes from the starting line up that beat Chelsea. The suspended Robert Huth is replaced by Marcin Wasilewski. In midfield, Andy King comes in for the injured Danny Drinkwater who is stood amongst the City fans in the upper tier of the Bullens Road stand. The only unenforced change sees

Shinji Okazaki recalled in place of Leonardo Ulloa up front.

Everton's attacking threat is built around three individuals: Romelu Lukaku, their leading goalscorer, Ross Barkley, their playmaker, and Gerard Deulofeu, their tricky wide player. Luckily for Ranieri, he has players in form who can snuff out each of these threats. Wes Morgan looks more like a leading Premier League centre-back with every game, N'Golo Kanté is quickly proving himself to be one of the best central midfielders in the country and Christian Fuchs appears to be one of the best free transfers in recent history.

The rain lashes down and the home side flood forward during a first half in which City must show grit and determination. Everton are winning the battle in midfield while Vardy and Okazaki are unable to hold the ball in attacking positions, resulting in one-way traffic towards Kasper Schmeichel. Roberto Martinez's side enjoy plenty of possession but struggle to fashion opportunities.

Last season, Everton would have scored twice before the break to effectively kill the game. Things are different this year and it's City who hit the front against the run of play. A Fuchs throw-in down the left is flicked on by Vardy to his strike partner Okazaki. The Everton centre-back Ramiro Funes Mori lets Okazaki past before hauling him to the ground near the byline. Referee Jonathan Moss correctly awards a penalty, which Riyad Mahrez scores at the Gwladys Street end.

The home fans are shocked but soon they are celebrating. Chaos in the City penalty area ends with Lukaku firing into an unguarded net to level the scores. Frustrating as it is, the goal is no more than Everton deserve for their greater enterprise.

In the second half, City begin to win key individual battles. Morgan handles Lukaku well. Kanté sticks close to Barkley. Deulofeu is getting little joy from Fuchs. All that remains is for City's own attacking talents to go and win the game. Halfway through the second half, the tide begins to turn.

Kanté collects the ball from King on the touchline, moves inside and finds Mahrez in space. Vardy runs in behind his England team-mate John Stones in anticipation of a through ball from Mahrez. Tim Howard rushes out and clips Vardy. Mahrez scores again from the spot.

Five minutes later, Marc Albrighton charges down a clearance by Seamus Coleman in Everton's right-back position, the ball breaks to Vardy who in turn finds Okazaki and the Japanese forward strikes a left-footed shot into the corner of Howard's net.

City lead by two goals with just twenty minutes to play of a fixture that was meant to be a real test of this team's credentials. Deulofeu is substituted and, while Kevin Mirallas does find a way past Schmeichel with a minute of normal time left to play, Everton can't find another goal in injury time.

As the 18.47 from Liverpool Lime Street pulls away from the platform, the songs can begin. We will be back in seven days for a Boxing Day clash at Anfield.

Liverpool and Everton remain ninth and tenth respectively after the Reds are beaten 3-0 by Watford at Vicarage Road, their fifth defeat of the season. City will return to Merseyside with optimism given Liverpool's mounting injury list, the brittle nature of their defence and their susceptibility to the counter attack.

On the Monday night following City's win at Goodison Park, second place plays third in north London as Manchester City travel to the Emirates Stadium to face Arsenal. The final Premier League game before Christmas is the latest in a long line of surreal milestones for Leicester City: our league position being affected by a match between the two title favourites in December. Decades have passed since the last time this happened.

Arsenal win 2-1 with goals from Theo Walcott and Olivier Giroud proving enough to render Yaya Toure's impressive late effort a consolation.

Everton 2 (Lukaku, Mirallas)
Leicester City 3 (Mahrez 2, Okazaki)
Team: Schmeichel, Simpson, Morgan, Wasilewski, Fuchs, Mahrez (De Laet), King, Kanté, Albrighton (Dyer), Okazaki, Vardy (Ulloa)

THE ICE KINGS

LEICESTER CITY FANS WAKE UP ON CHRISTMAS MORNING AND check the Premier League table. Yes, it's still looking as surreal as it did yesterday and the day before that and every week since the season began.

Leicester City are top of the Premier League, twelve months after sitting bottom of the table. We are the first team to achieve this feat in the Premier League era and only the second, after Norwich City in 1988, in the history of English football.

For a number of weeks, BBC Radio Leicester have been playing the Champions League theme tune to open their Monday night football phone-in. It started out as a bit of a joke but there's a real chance that it will be heard at the King Power next season. City are nine points clear of fifth place and have lost only one of the first seventeen games.

Christmas Day comes and goes. We eat too much, maybe we drink too much, and we talk about the miracle taking place. We wake up the following morning and we can't wait to see our team again, like thousands of City fans just over fifty years ago.

Boxing Day 1962. Leicester City were an established First Division team, having lost in the FA Cup Final to the famous double-winning Tottenham Hotspur side just eighteen months before. In wintry conditions, City beat Leyton Orient 5-1 at Filbert Street. This was one of many defeats for Orient during the course of what remains their only season in the top flight. City, on the other hand, were just getting started.

The whole of Britain was paralysed by arctic weather but, as other teams up and down the country postponed their games week after week, Leicester City played on.

In those days, John Hutchinson used to pay seven and a half pence to stand on the Popular Side at Filbert Street and peer through gaps in the crowd to see his heroes. He never even expected to see the whole pitch. Now, in his role as the club's official historian, he knows an awful lot more about it.

'One of the reasons they kept playing was because the groundsman had some chemical mixture he put on the grass,' says Hutchinson. 'It kept the pitch warm but it ruined it for years to come. They also had coke braziers they used to light and then remove four hours before kick-off.'

It's a world away from the state-of-the-art playing surface at the King Power Stadium, artificial grass sewn into the soil and maintained by an award-winning team led by head groundsman John Ledwidge.

In the winter of 1962/63, the pitch didn't need to win awards. It just needed to be playable.

'When other teams came, they weren't used to the surface,' says Hutchinson. 'Leicester were a great side anyway, but they also knew how to play on the pitch and it gave them an edge.'

That edge resulted in a long line of victories and the birth of a nickname: 'The Ice Kings'. City won ten games in a row – seven in the league and three in the FA Cup – before Tottenham managed a 2-2 draw on 23 March 1963.

There were plenty of rearranged games to fit in though, leading to fixture congestion that would terrify the players and managers of today. Remarkably, City faced Manchester United at Old Trafford on 15 April and the return fixture was played the following day.

Nearly 40,000 fans packed into Filbert Street for the visit of United before the doors were locked and some supporters were reduced to waiting in the terraced streets outside, listening intently for the roar of those inside.

Another young City fan, John Wright, was one of the unlucky ones.

'My brother had managed to get in but I was outside in a crowd around the exit gates where people were sitting on the wall and telling us what was happening,' he says. 'There seemed to be a few hundred or more but it's difficult to say as going to the football was a completely new experience for me, never mind being locked out.'

Unfortunately, he missed a classic.

Despite struggling in the league, United had stars like Bobby Charlton and Denis Law in their side. Law scored a hat-trick, including an exceptional bicycle kick, but it was in vain. City top goalscorer Ken Keyworth's own hat-trick at the other end took just six minutes as the game ended 4-3 to City.

The Ice Kings were top of the table with five league games and one FA Cup semi-final remaining. Four days after seeing off United, a 1-1 draw with Wolverhampton Wanderers was a setback but the chance of glory remained.

Those who remember the early 1960s are able to reel off the team with little hesitation: Banks, Sjoberg, Norman, McLintock, King, Appleton, Riley, Cross, Keyworth, Gibson, Stringfellow.

Today's team is similarly settled and will also be remembered as a collective for years to come: Schmeichel, Simpson, Huth, Morgan, Fuchs, Albrighton, Drinkwater, Kanté, Mahrez, Okazaki, Vardy.

Davie Gibson was magical, the artist, the creator who made City tick with his skill and invention, the Mahrez of the Ice Kings, but the real similarity was in the counter-attacking style of play, an approach that did not go unnoticed when City lined up against Bill Shankly's Liverpool at Hillsborough for their FA Cup semi-final. The management team of Matt Gillies and Bert Johnson were renowned for their tactical innovation, with Graham Cross and Frank McLintock swapping places while other sides stuck rigidly to a 2-3-5 formation.

Club historian Hutchinson has spoken to several of the Ice Kings about the lessons Liverpool learned that afternoon.

'They all told me that Shankly criticised the way Leicester played in the semi-final,' he says. 'The following season though, he adopted the same tactics which I think is quite an accolade.'

City beat Liverpool 1-0 to reach the final but perhaps the prospect of the big day ahead at Wembley acted as a distraction. The final four league games of the season all ended in defeat and the team finished in fourth place.

Still, they were red hot favourites to win the FA Cup against a Manchester United side that had just finished fourth bottom of the league.

The final score was Manchester United 3 Leicester City 1.

'Losing in the cup final has stuck with me more than the league failure,' says John Wright. 'Perhaps that's because we were favourites right up to the kick-off.

'I've always wanted to win the FA Cup – maybe because it seemed more achievable, because of the past failures, or simply because I'm a tad envious that a club of our standing has never won it when even the likes of Coventry and Wigan have done.

'I've never really thought about winning the league. Certainly not in recent memory and due to past near misses I don't like to think about it. After all, it wasn't that long ago that we were a team winning 3-0 at half time that went on to lose 4-3. For most of my time supporting Leicester, that has been nearer the norm than winning.

'If we were to win the league, I think I could retire happily from attending City games. My wife has always wanted to live on the coast.'

For Hutchinson, the opportunity to meet and interview heroes from his child-hood has been a privilege and he is thrilled by how this season is panning out. The current side's success has brought the Ice Kings back into the spotlight but now the question is whether City can complete that final step of the journey.

'People are excited,' says Hutchinson. 'The place is buzzing because the global interest in the club is phenomenal. A lot of people have been here for several years and have seen everything from relegation to League One through to where we are now.

'The people who work here are Leicester City supporters. There's excitement. There's disbelief. There's also caution.

'Until I went to university in 1967, I just always assumed Leicester City were a top side. When they went down in 1969 it was a huge shock. I was lucky as a fan growing up in the 1960s because they had some great players: Banks, McLintock, Gibson, Dougan, Sinclair, Clarke, Rodrigues, Shilton, Nish.

'It's great now to be back to where we were then. It brings back how I felt when I was a kid. This is fantastic. We're at the top. This is special.'

18: LIVERPOOL (A)

Saturday 26 December 2015

FOR THE LAST AWAY GAME OF 2015, WE RETURN TO THE VENUE of the first. On New Year's Day, City battled adversity to secure a 2-2 draw at Anfield. Nigel Pearson was in charge and the goals came from David Nugent and Jeff Schlupp. The current stars of City's attack – Jamie Vardy and Riyad Mahrez – were relegated to supporting roles, each claiming an assist in an excellent team performance.

Vardy and Mahrez are two of just four players to start both league games at Anfield in 2015, along with Wes Morgan and Danny Simpson, who each conceded dubious penalties in the first fixture. Ranieri is hoping for better luck than Pearson got that afternoon.

Robert Huth returns from suspension in place of Marcin Wasilewski, who performed well in the German's absence. Danny Drinkwater remains unavailable through injury. Shinji Okazaki retains his place up front ahead of Leonardo Ulloa.

Liverpool have continued to under-perform this season despite the appointment of the much-coveted former Borussia Dortmund manager Jürgen Klopp, their form varying between the high of a 4-1 win at Manchester City and the low of a 3-0 defeat at newly-promoted Watford the weekend before Christmas.

Unfortunately for City, the Reds look in the mood on Boxing Day and tear into Ranieri's men from the outset. Our players look uncharacteristically sloppy, surrendering possession throughout a disappointing first half. Whether as a result of Liverpool's energetic pressing game or too much turkey on Christmas Day, the ball constantly passes from blue to red.

The only positives are the performance of N'Golo Kanté and the fact City somehow go in at the break with the game still goalless. While the mood in the away end doesn't reach January's levels of despondency when Liverpool were 2-0 up and City looked destined for relegation, there is a sense of disappointment. This team seemed perfectly set up to win at places like Anfield. That's not going to happen today.

There shouldn't be too much doom and gloom. In July, Roberto Firmino became Liverpool's second most expensive player of all time when he arrived from Hoffenheim for a fee rising to £29million. Two weeks later, Christian Benteke pushed Firmino down a place in the list after signing from Aston Villa for £32.5million. So it's over £60million of talent that combines to produce the only goal of the game. Firmino gets the ball across from the left and Benteke strays from Huth before guiding his shot past Kasper Schmeichel.

The game ends in bizarre circumstances. Schmeichel is caught out of his goal after heading upfield for an injury time City corner and Liverpool break with four players bearing down on the retreating Wes Morgan. Benteke contrives to strike the ball into Morgan and the chance is lost. City swiftly counter attack. Marc Albrighton bursts down the right and crosses for Andy King whose header loops slowly onto the roof of the net. We slump to our seats as the referee Martin Atkinson blows his whistle, marking City's first league defeat away from home since losing at Tottenham Hotspur in March.

That sums up one of the biggest challenges for this remarkable team during the rest of the season. In the period between those two defeats, we didn't have to travel to any of the six current Premier League teams that have ever qualified for the Champions League group stages: Arsenal, Chelsea, Liverpool, Manchester City, Manchester United and Tottenham.

While that means five of the toughest fixtures of the season lie in the remaining twenty games, the brevity of that list also shows just what a staggering achievement it would be for a seventh club to be added in May. There are few teams in the mix: Crystal Palace, West Ham United, Watford and Stoke City among them. Leicester City remain in pole position.

Liverpool 1 (Benteke)
Leicester City 0
Team: Schmeichel, Simpson, Morgan, Huth, Fuchs, Mahrez (Kramarić), King,
Kanté, Albrighton, Okazaki (Dyer), Vardy (Ulloa)

THE AUSSIE

FOR GLENN BRADBURY, IT HASN'T ALWAYS BEEN EASY TO
follow Leicester City.

'Dad brought us to Australia in the 1970s,' says Glenn. 'Before the days of the
internet, the BBC reports on a Sunday morning and week-old copies of Shoot or
Scorcher magazine were the only ways to keep up with how City were getting on.'

Fast forward forty years and the fragile nature of City's Premier League status
at the end of the 2014/15 season meant Glenn thought the following campaign
might represent his only chance to see his team in the top flight. The price looked
prohibitive but his wife Nic gave the trip the go-ahead.

'Work prevented me from travelling at times other than Christmas and when the
fixtures came out, I was equally thrilled and terrified,' he says. 'We bought the plane
tickets before the season began and, in all honesty, I thought that if I even saw us
score just one goal in four games, that would be enough. Chelsea would win without
us scoring. Maybe we would sneak a goal at Everton. Liverpool would probably stick
a couple past us and maybe we could hold onto a goalless draw against Manchester
City.'

The next obstacle was one that has caused problems even to local City fans.

'I asked online if anyone could help with tickets,' says Glenn. 'How funny would
it be that I get over and then can't see any of the games? Fortunately I was able to
get tickets for all the games from Gaz, one of the regulars in the Union FS section.
I couldn't thank him enough.

'I had arranged to meet Gaz at the turnstiles to collect my tickets. As I stood
there, I realised that this could be a complete disaster. What if he didn't turn up?
What if he had no tickets and he was just standing somewhere laughing and I would
be stuck in England with hotels booked across the country but no tickets. That was
a nervy few minutes! Of course he did turn up and the tickets were sorted.'

A lot had changed between the fixtures being announced in the summer and the
day of the home clash with Chelsea. City were second in the league.

'I was amazed,' says Glenn. 'But we hadn't played many of the so-called big teams yet, so the crash was near and inevitable. My hope had now changed to maybe just once in my life I would be able to sing 'we're top of the league'. All it needed was City to score first against Chelsea and my dreams would be answered.

'I was lucky enough to be a part of the Union FS area, which was incredibly loud all game. Then came the moment I'll never forget. I can just close my eyes and watch that moment of Mahrez magic time and time again. Then the roar, the surge of joy and the singing about being top of the league. Just unbelievable.

'The win against Chelsea had exceeded my hopes and being in the away end at a beautiful old ground like Goodison the following Saturday when we won was perfection.'

The feast of football was interrupted briefly by the arrival of Christmas. Glenn and Nic went off to Wales to 'see something touristy' and headed back to England.

'To our horror we discovered that nothing was open on Christmas Day,' says Glenn. 'Nothing! So our Christmas lunch was some leftover lettuce on a couple of crusts in the driveway of an industrial estate just outside Runcorn.'

The loss at Liverpool, while disappointing, was expected, and Glenn was just thrilled to be among the City fans outsinging Anfield.

'After forty years in Australia, I now have a very broad Aussie accent so I can sound wrong when I start singing,' he says. 'It took some careful thought as I sang to ensure the Leicester accent overwhelmed the Oz drawl. Loss or no loss, I was still proud of the lads and proud of our fans.

'Just before we were due to leave for the UK, we learned of the change to the Manchester City game's kick-off time. This was a disaster. It meant that I wouldn't be able to see the game as I would be on the plane flying home.

'Incredibly though, the plane had live television coverage of the game so I sat and watched the game.'

As Glenn prepared to watch on at 30,000 feet, another 30,000 City fans took their place at the King Power Stadium for one of the most difficult games of the season.

19: MANCHESTER CITY (H)

Tuesday 29 December 2015

MANCHESTER CITY'S STARTING ELEVEN FOR THE KING POWER Stadium's final Premier League match of 2015 costs just under £300million. The expectations of their owners, their supporters, the media and the opposition are sky high every time they take to the pitch. You don't get to field an extra man though no matter how much you spend and Claudio Ranieri can reasonably expect his own players can win their individual battles to offer a chance of victory.

To the media and most neutrals, of course, Manchester City are 'City'. No other City had ever won the title and the last City to finish second in the top flight was Leicester in 1929.

For us, there is only one City and they play in royal blue.

Ranieri makes two changes to the side beaten by Liverpool three days ago. Gökhan Inler makes only his third league start of the season in a three-man central midfield alongside N'Golo Kanté and the returning Danny Drinkwater, a much-missed presence at Anfield.

We're treated to free bottles of beer by the club's owners for our support throughout the year and we're in full voice prior to kick-off.

The match quickly takes on a predictable pattern with Ranieri's men retreating to the edge of the penalty area while Manchester City set about making pretty passing patterns in front of them. Manuel Pellegrini opts for 4-4-2 with Sergio Agüero joined in attack by Raheem Sterling, but their efforts are met with fierce resistance and Kasper Schmeichel easily repels attempts from Sterling and Kevin de Bruyne.

It's the £1 million striker at the other end of the pitch who should open the scoring. Fernandinho is hesitant in possession and Jamie Vardy nips in. Drinkwater plays a sharp through ball and Vardy is through. Perhaps he would have fired into the net during his famous goalscoring run but he skies this shot over the bar and the two highest-scoring sides in the Premier League this season return to their dressing rooms goalless.

The second half is equally devoid of incident, save for an Agüero penalty appeal as a result of a mis-timed challenge by Inler. Referee Craig Pawson turns down Agüero's request and his number is up. He wanders off the field bemused by the decision and with him goes any attacking threat from the visitors. Wilfried Bony is Agüero's replacement – a man who scored twice against City last season in the white of Swansea but who has failed to fire since moving to Manchester. Wes Morgan and Robert Huth dealt well with Agüero and they see off Bony as well.

Defenders are on top all over the pitch. Even Vardy is kept under control by Manchester City's unheralded centre-backs Eliaquim Mangala and Nicolas Otamendi after the break, bringing the visitors their first clean sheet without captain Vincent Kompany. Ranieri brings Leonardo Ulloa on for Inler to offer support to Vardy but there's nothing doing.

The kamikaze approach to Arsenal's visit back in September feels a long time ago. That game fizzed for ninety minutes. This one fizzles out, but the mood is brighter. The six games meant to test this supposedly threadbare squad have resulted in three wins, two draws and one solitary defeat.

The final light goes out at the King Power Stadium after a year of highs, lows, beginnings, endings and a quite incredible turnaround in fortunes.

Inside these four walls, we have seen the first tifos, the rise of Union FS, Andy King sparking the greatest escape of all, Esteban Cambiasso's farewell bow, Nigel Pearson's final game in charge of Leicester, José Mourinho's final game in charge of Chelsea, the arrival of new heroes: Claudio Ranieri; N'Golo Kanté; Robert Huth; Christian Fuchs, and one of the most remarkable goals in the club's history: Jamie Vardy's record-breaking strike against Manchester United.

How does 2016 begin to top that?

Leicester City 0
Manchester City 0
Team: Schmeichel, Simpson, Morgan, Huth, Fuchs, Mahrez, Inler (Ulloa),
Drinkwater (King), Kanté, Albrighton (De Laet), Vardy

THE GREAT DANE

AS THEY PREPARE TO LEAVE THE PITCH AFTER THE GOALLESS draw between their two sides, Kasper Schmeichel and Joe Hart – friends, former team-mates and fellow international number ones – embrace and share a joke. Perhaps Hart is complimenting his opposite number for the fine save from Raheem Sterling that helped to secure a point.

It's a satisfying end to the year for Schmeichel, a year he began injured. In fact, his first game back from a three-month absence was the 4-3 defeat by Tottenham Hotspur at White Hart Lane in March that seemingly jolted Leicester City into action prior to the great escape.

Schmeichel is one of City's longest-serving players, having signed from Leeds United at the age of 24 in the summer of 2011. Some Leeds fans told us at the time they were upgrading between the sticks by replacing Schmeichel with Andy Lonergan. There was even speculation the Dane was forced out of Elland Road and reluctant to move to City. What a wise move it looks now, with Leeds struggling in the Championship while City continue to confound expectations in the top flight.

Captain Wes Morgan says he regularly calls on the expertise of both Schmeichel and Andy King, and it bodes well for the club's long-term future that leaders among the playing staff have been around long enough to truly understand and connect with the fanbase.

In the five years since his arrival, outfield players have come and gone but our number one goalkeeper has always been the same.

There has been no room for error and any doubters have now been converted. Schmeichel is one of the most improved players in the squad. Question marks over his command of the penalty area and susceptibility to high crosses have disappeared, whether through better technique or communication.

The tightened back four helps, without question, but Schmeichel has developed into one of the best goalkeepers in the Premier League.

20: AFC BOURNEMOUTH (H)

Saturday 2 January 2016

BUMP.

Bump.

Bump. Bump. Bump.

2016 opens with the sound of Leicester City fans being brought back down to earth. Halfway through a surreal dream world of a season, here's a rare, bitter dose of reality. This is what football used to feel like. This is what football should feel like. In a word, frustrating.

Bournemouth aren't scared of anyone. They play attractively and expansively, switching play from one side of the pitch to the other with confidence despite the obvious threat of the famous City counter-attack. Eddie Howe's team waste two clear chances in an open first half. Josh King heads wide as Kasper Schmeichel scrambles desperately across his goal line. Shortly after, Dan Gosling fires the ball way over Schmeichel's crossbar when well placed.

The visitors should be ahead and they're relieved when Jamie Vardy fires one chance high into the Family Stand and cracks another against the post from four yards.

There's still an expectant atmosphere, because trips to White Hart Lane, the Etihad and the Emirates loom on the horizon. We don't want our players to let this one get away.

The game changes after an hour with the familiar sight of Vardy making a cartoon villain dash towards goal at the Kop end with a set of opposition defenders giving chase like overweight policemen.

We look set for a smash-and-grab to match the trip to Bournemouth in August when we looted a point. That day, Steve Cook tripped the onrushing Vardy and the striker belted the resulting spot kick into the top corner. This time Cook can only watch as his team-mate Simon Francis sends Vardy to the ground inside the box and, despite protracted protests, is sent off.

Riyad Mahrez is City's designated penalty taker. We need him to smash the ball into the net like Vardy did. Instead, Mahrez stutters in his run-up and his weak effort is easily repelled by Bournemouth goalkeeper Artur Boruc.

It's okay. City have half an hour to get a winner against a newly-promoted team playing with ten men.

But it's not okay. Our heroes labour to create chances and waste the ones they do fashion. When a corner travels all the way to the far post and Wes Morgan scoops a shot into the crowd from underneath the crossbar, one fan in the Kop catches the ball and thousands more let out a resigned sigh.

This game will end goalless.

Leicester City 0

AFC Bournemouth 0

Team: Schmeichel, Simpson (De Laet), Morgan, Huth, Fuchs, Albrighton (Okazaki), Drinkwater, Kanté, Mahrez, Ulloa (Dyer), Vardy

THE BRUMMIE BLUE

ACCORDING TO THE BBC, EDDIE HOWE'S AFC BOURNEMOUTH had four bids rejected for Birmingham City winger Demarai Gray in January 2015. Gray is not for sale at any price, the Championship club are told.

Since then, Bournemouth have been promoted to the Premier League as champions and enjoyed an impressive start to life in the top flight.

Following their 0-0 draw at the King Power Stadium, a year on from those rejected bids, Gray finally leaves Birmingham. He doesn't head to the south coast though.

Demarai Gray signs for Leicester City. He wants to be part of a story beginning to captivate the world. Bournemouth weren't the only club linked with Gray. Liverpool, Tottenham and Southampton were among those reported to show interest. He has been scouted and monitored by the biggest clubs in English football. Leicester City made the decisive move.

Gray's performance in the final pre-season fixture prior to the 2015/16 season was a factor. Birmingham already led 1-0 when the ball was played out to the left wing. Gray took a touch to control and faced up to Marc Albrighton. One little shimmy as he moved into the penalty area at an acute angle and he hit it. The ball flew into the top corner past Kasper Schmeichel's despairing dive.

The Birmingham fans celebrated as though this was a league game. Here was their brightest young prospect showing a Premier League team how it was done. There was immense pride in those celebrations.

On the touchline, Claudio Ranieri made a mental note and watched as his team battled back to win the game.

'I watched some matches before playing against Birmingham,' said Ranieri after welcoming Gray to the club. 'Already I saw he was very good but when we played against him I thought: he is fantastic.'

Pre-season feels a long time ago as winter takes grip. With Riyad Mahrez and Marc Albrighton off-form and showing signs of fatigue, the arrival of an exciting winger to push for their places is perfectly timed – just like the summer strike that made us sit up and take notice of Demarai Gray.

21: TOTTENHAM HOTSPUR (A)

Wednesday 13 January 2016

THIS IS THE TIPPING POINT. EXACTLY SIX MONTHS HAVE PASSED since an Italian took a job. Now we're balancing on the edge of a clifftop road in the Alps. The gold bars are at one end of the bus and we're at the other. Do we get the gold? Or are we about to plunge?

We travel to a chilly White Hart Lane for the second time in four days. Three days earlier, a very different side battled to a 2-2 draw in the FA Cup. It took a controversial late penalty to deny City outright victory after coming from behind to lead. Marcin Wasilewski and Shinji Okazaki were the goalscorers, while new signing Demarai Gray impressed on his debut.

Claudio Ranieri reverts to his preferred Premier League starting eleven and the game begins in familiar fashion. Tottenham retain possession and spread the ball wide to their overlapping full-backs. City drop deep with two banks of four sweeping across the pitch from side to side. On the touchline, Ranieri whistles, holds his hands out in front of him with palms facing and pushes them towards each other like he's miming pottery. Compact. Compact. Shape. Shape.

The manager is adding defensive solidity to City's devil-may-care instinct, as he said he would when he arrived: 'the Italian tactical way' as Ranieri called it in one of his first interviews. We were worried he would restrict the more attack-minded players in the squad. That didn't happen at first but a defensive mindset is creeping in.

We get the rub of the green, most notably when Harry Kane breaks clear of Wes Morgan for the one and only time. Kane shoots and Kasper Schmeichel gets a hand to the ball, sending it down into the turf and up onto the crossbar. It bounces away to safety and Kane momentarily has good reason for his perennial expression of disbelief. The Tottenham supporters surely begin to think this isn't their night. And they'd be right.

After 83 minutes of dogged defensive work, we come to the moment that changes the complexion of this incredible season.

The tireless N'Golo Kanté grafts away to win a corner, which Christian Fuchs delivers to the far post. From high up in the away end, we watch as Robert Huth trots into space. He doesn't even need to jump. Huth draws back his neck and then sends it forward at force, his forehead making a clean connection with the ball and sending it arrowing high over Tottenham's beanpole goalkeeper Hugo Lloris.

It took tremendous accuracy for City to find a way past the Frenchman back in August when Riyad Mahrez's powerful drive found the far corner of the net. It takes another inch-perfect effort to beat him again. Ben Davies springs towards the ball but fails to head it off the line and it crashes into the net.

Pandemonium among the sold-out visitors' section that the bear-like Huth jogs towards with arms outstretched, having scooped Drinkwater and Mahrez up with each of his giant paws. In fact, the rest of the City players look like children celebrating with their father. And this on a school night.

Tottenham push forward in search of an equaliser but they fail to force any clear chances. City see out the game in reasonable comfort. Substitutes Leonardo Ulloa and Andy King may not be the quickest but their steadfast touches and clever hold-up play ensure a crucial victory.

The result is overshadowed in the media by a televised 3-3 draw between Liverpool and Arsenal at Anfield, but that suits City just fine. Anything that takes the pressure away from Ranieri's band of fighters is a welcome distraction. Joe Allen's last-minute equaliser for Liverpool means City draw level with Arsenal on 43 points.

Of course every game is difficult and you never truly come to the end of a tough run in the Premier League until the final day but many saw City's fixture list over Christmas and New Year as particularly daunting. Defeat was avoided against both Manchester clubs before the reigning champions were downed and all three points were taken from Goodison Park and White Hart Lane.

The Tottenham High Road, glistening in the aftermath of the rain that fell during the second half, is closed after the match. We're tempted to dance through the puddles and twirl round the lampposts but there's no time to be Gene Kelly tonight. Instead, we've got to shuffle into queues on the platforms of Seven Sisters and Northumberland Park and smile surreptitiously among a legion of frustrated Cockneys. We're grinning in the rain.

Tottenham Hotspur 0
Leicester City 1 (Huth)
Team: Schmeichel, Simpson, Morgan, Huth, Fuchs, Mahrez (Dyer),
Drinkwater, Kanté, Albrighton, Okazaki (King), Vardy (Ulloa)

THE SEXY FOOTBALL SHOW

ROBERT HUTH IS CARVED OUT OF GRANITE. HE'S LIKE AN EASTER Island statue. He's a colossus. He was the answer to Leicester City's defensive problems last season and he's the answer to our goalscoring problem at White Hart Lane. With Jamie Vardy still recovering from a groin operation and Riyad Mahrez suffering a slight dip in form, Huth steps into the breach and nabs one of the most important goals of the season.

Keeps his eye on the ball. Leans back. Neck muscles. Oomph.

We are so lucky to have Robert Huth. Sometimes the best signings aren't planned for months. They just fall into your lap. Huth fell into ours and after we had winced from the impact, we smiled. As he said himself on Twitter, the sexy football show had rolled into town. Stoke let him go last summer following his valuable contribution on loan at the King Power and we thanked them very much.

It is said that the likes of Huth and Wes Morgan are old-fashioned. Old school. Just old. The trend is for younger, more athletic £30million centre-backs who can't defend. City spent £3million on one who doesn't just defend. He loves defending.

Chuck the ball in our box. Go on. Oomph. Out it goes. Try again. Oomph. Sorry, that was no good either.

Huth clearly pushes the boundaries. The laws of the game are stretched to within a hair's breadth of their most lenient application, but football is a contact sport and this team is built on a competitive edge. We take the rough with the smooth. We take all three points from White Hart Lane.

22: ASTON VILLA (A)

Saturday 16 January 2016

ON VALENTINE'S DAY 2015, LEICESTER CITY MADE THE SHORT trip south west to Birmingham to face Aston Villa in the FA Cup fifth round. That encounter marked one of the lowest points of a season that wasn't short on depressing away days. The great escape was just a distant dream at that stage and we suffered the indignity of watching a dreadful performance in a demoralising defeat televised live to millions of viewers.

So much has changed. That is to say, City are top of the league once the final whistle sounds at Villa Park. The performance, unfortunately, is arguably the worst of the campaign. There's more attacking threat than there was eleven months ago but we also see concerning signs – wasted opportunities; sloppy passes; overly aggressive defending.

Robert Huth should concede a penalty. Riyad Mahrez misses one. Jamie Vardy doesn't look match fit. Mahrez looks tired. None of it should matter. City are top of the league. And yet. What an opportunity this season is presenting. As the media keep saying, 'nobody wants to win the league.' It's not even necessarily about the title. The Champions League, though. It's right there in front of us and it's making some of us feel incredibly spoilt.

As the City players make their way across to the away section, there are hundreds of supporters already filing out into the chilly west Midlands night.

Almost everything has gone right so far this season, particularly the substitutions made by Claudio Ranieri. The wily old fox seems to have a knack. So when he removes Shinji Okazaki, City's goalscorer and most effective player, early in the second half and replaces him with right-back Ritchie De Laet, there are one or two alarm bells. Is this the first sign of the dreaded 'Tinkerman', the nickname Ranieri earned during his time at Chelsea for a propensity to make strange changes?

We haven't worked out our team's place in the grand order of things yet. To be top after a handful of games was nice. To be joint top in the middle of January is something else entirely. It could be the beginning of something special, or it could be the zenith of this club's achievement for years.

We're soon forced to concentrate on the league after a one-sided FA Cup fourth round replay dominated by visitors Tottenham Hotspur. The last of three games in quick succession against the Londoners ends in a 2-0 defeat after goals in each half from Heung-Min Son and Nacer Chadli.

Aston Villa 1 (Gestede)
Leicester City 1 (Okazaki)
Team: Schmeichel, Simpson, Morgan, Huth, Fuchs, Mahrez (Ulloa), Drinkwater, Kanté, Albrighton (Gray), Okazaki (De Laet), Vardy

THE RUN

FROM THE HUNDREDS OF VIDEO CLIPS OUR UNPARALLELED scouting team trawled through in their deliberation over whether to recommend the signing of Daniel Amartey, one in particular must have stood out.

6 October 2013: Five minutes of injury time were coming to an end and less than sixty seconds remained in the Swedish league meeting between Djurgårdens and IFK Göteborg as the ball sailed over the halfway line. The score was 1-1. The retreating Djurgårdens defender Amartey, an 18-year-old Ghanaian in his first season at professional level, was almost caught out by the bounce of the ball.

94:14 - He managed to stop running towards his own goal just in time to leap into the air and chest the ball away from an onrushing Göteborg attacker, turning to his left outside the penalty area.

Amartey took a touch and passed the ball out to a team-mate on the right wing.

Then he set off, sprinting through the centre circle at breakneck speed.

His team-mate had sauntered forward before knocking the ball on to the edge of the Göteborg box.

94:24 - Imperceptibly, Amartey was there. He nudged the ball past the eighteen-yard line only to be wiped out by a challenge from an opposition defender.

In ten seconds, Amartey had taken Djurgårdens from a position of danger at one end to winning a penalty at the other.

Djurgårdens scored the penalty to win 2-1 in the 96th minute.

Amartey moved on to FC Copenhagen in Denmark in 2014 and made his international debut the following year, becoming part of the Ghana squad that finished runners-up in the 2015 Africa Cup of Nations in Equatorial Guinea.

Leicester City parted with a reported £6million to bring Amartey to the King Power Stadium ahead of the home game with Stoke City, where he aimed to play a part in his new club's pursuit of European football.

23: STOKE CITY (H)

Saturday 23 January 2016

LET'S DO THIS WEEKEND BACK TO FRONT. ON SUNDAY AFTERNOON, a battling Chelsea performance means defeat for Arsenal leaving them on 44 points from 23 games. They fall beneath Manchester City in the table after Manuel Pellegrini's side come from behind twice to draw 2-2 at West Ham in Saturday's late kick-off thanks to two Sergio Agüero goals.

But what of Leicester City?

Stoke manager Mark Hughes has one eye on the impending League Cup semi-final second leg at Anfield so his side is missing Bojan Krkic and Marko Arnautovic, arguably their two best attacking players, who combined to produce the opening goal in City's 2-2 draw at the Britannia Stadium in September. City's goalscorers that day, Riyad Mahrez and Jamie Vardy, have struggled for form and fitness since Christmas.

What the home fans want to see most of all is a committed, attacking display. The goals have dried up. The pressing has stopped. The question on the lips of everyone in the media is whether the bubble is about to burst.

Thankfully, the answer is an emphatic no. City win.

Victory comes via Danny Drinkwater's first ever Premier League goal, a welcome return to the scoresheet for Vardy – his first goal in over ten hours – and a redemptive strike from substitute Leonardo Ulloa.

Most importantly, we see the return of relentless pressing from the front, with Vardy and Shinji Okazaki chugging away to disrupt the visitors' passing game. Drinkwater and N'Golo Kanté, both of whom looked subdued in the previous league outing at Villa Park, are back to their best. Stoke might enjoy 55% of the possession but their central midfielders, Ibrahim Afellay and Glenn Whelan, are dominated by City's dynamic duo. The Potters manage just three shots in the entire game and only one of those, a free header for the Spanish forward Josélu with City leading 1-0, feels like a wasted opportunity.

That chance arrived after 61 minutes and Vardy scores the second City goal just five minutes later. Drinkwater lofts a through ball with his weaker foot and Vardy gets away from Marc Wilson, a first-half substitute following injury to the influential Stoke captain Ryan Shawcross. England's newest striker faces England's newest goalkeeper, the talented youngster Jack Butland, but the number nine holds the advantage. Vardy skilfully rounds Butland. For the second time this season, he guides the ball into the corner of Butland's net. Back in September, it secured a point. Now it secures all three.

The third goal is poked in by Ulloa following outrageous skill from Mahrez to send the ball between the legs of Stoke defender Philipp Wollscheid. One for the end-of-season highlights reels.

Arsenal and Manchester City's inability to win, coupled with a 1-0 defeat for Manchester United at home to Southampton, leaves a three-point gap to second place and a yawning ten-point chasm beyond the final Champions League spot to fifth-placed United.

The final weekend of January is reserved for a City-less FA Cup fourth round so Ranieri's troops will remain top of the Premier League into February. But hours before the visit of Liverpool on the second day of the second month, the transfer window closes. Even a comprehensive 3-0 win – and goals for Vardy and Ulloa – can't disguise the widespread clamour for a new forward. Andrej Kramarić has been allowed to join Bundesliga side Hoffenheim on loan for the rest of the season, meaning just three recognised strikers remain in the squad.

City signed winger Demarai Gray from Birmingham City, then added defensive utility man Daniel Amartey from FC Copenhagen and Claudio Ranieri states that he will sign another attacking player before the window closes.

But he doesn't.

And we pray it won't cost us.

Leicester City 3 (Drinkwater, Vardy, Ulloa)

Stoke City 0

Team: Schmeichel, Simpson, Morgan, Huth, Fuchs, Mahrez, Drinkwater, Kanté, Albrighton (Gray), Okazaki (Ulloa), Vardy

THE DYNAMIC DUO

THE JANUARY TRANSFER WINDOW CLOSES TO LEAVE LEICESTER City relying on three recognised strikers in the final few months of the season.

It seems a risk. Reinforcements in forward areas had been pursued but none arrived.

We'll have to go with what we've got. Thankfully, that's the best squad we've ever had.

We had been concerned this squad would disintegrate when Nigel Pearson left the previous summer and many supporters had hung their hopes of continuity on the retention of assistant managers Craig Shakespeare and Steve Walsh.

We feared Pearson would walk into another job and take his long-time friends and associates with him. But that job didn't materialise. Shakespeare and Walsh stayed, sharing their expertise with Claudio Ranieri and the new members of staff that arrived with him.

Shakespeare's presence on the training ground appears a key element in maintaining the bond that existed between the players and coaching staff during Pearson's time in charge. He can also be seen deep in conversation with Ranieri on the touchline during matches, often prior to a key tactical switch or substitution that swings the game in City's favour.

Walsh, who leads the club's enviable scouting setup, is the man credited with discovering Riyad Mahrez in French second division side Le Havre's midfield and repeatedly implored Ranieri to sign N'Golo Kanté. Managers often become the individual focus for supporters and receive credit for success as well as carrying the can after failure and Walsh receives the same treatment, frequently lauded for the work of his department.

The only difference is how rarely he fails. Other clubs have pinched members of Walsh's staff – Rob Mackenzie went to Tottenham Hotspur in February 2015 and Ben Wrigglesworth is on the verge of moving to Arsenal at the closure of this transfer window – but the good work continues.

That work shows quality rather than quantity. We had wanted a striker, but as we prepare to face Liverpool, Manchester City and Arsenal – 'the big rocks', as Ranieri calls them - maybe all the pieces of the jigsaw are already in place.

24: LIVERPOOL (H)

Tuesday 2 February 2016

IT WAS A LIVERPOOL MANAGER, OF COURSE, WHO SAID THAT football was more important than life and death. It isn't. It's only a game. But what a game it can be. What else in life can give you a moment like the one we experienced at 9.00pm on Tuesday 2 February 2016?

Riyad Mahrez wins a 50/50 halfway inside the City half and quickly sends the ball over sixty yards upfield, a glorious lofted through ball that isolates Jamie Vardy one-on-one with an opposition defender. Dejan Lovren prepares to try to prevent the Premier League's leading goalscorer running through on goal.

It's perfectly understandable that central defenders don't want to get too tight to Vardy because the City striker's acceleration can be frightening. Lovren stands off him a little, but this is the one time Vardy decides not to run on towards goal. Instead, he spots the Liverpool goalkeeper Simon Mignolet off his line as the ball bounces and drops and Vardy swings his right boot at it. The arc of the ball is beautiful. It soars over Mignolet before dipping under the crossbar into the net.

The roar is deafening.

In an instant, the transfer window is forgotten. The penalty misses in drawn matches against Bournemouth and Aston Villa are forgotten. The groin operation that kept Vardy out of the recent FA Cup game at Tottenham is certainly forgotten. He's striding towards the corner flag while commentators all over the world are screaming at their viewers and listeners. Goal! Gol! Gooooooooolazo!

Vardy adds another goal eleven minutes later and City see out the game in comfort. Liverpool are beaten to avenge the 1-0 reverse at Anfield on Boxing Day, one of only two league defeats so far this season. 24 games played. 14 games won. 50 points in the bag. Three points clear of Manchester City at the top of the table.

From the outside, it appears that City have reverted to a good old-fashioned 4-4-2 in an age where so many managers are overthinking the tactical side of the game and ending up with imbalanced line ups. This game is the perfect example. City have the ball for just one-third of the game but convert that into three times as many shots on target as the visitors.

Liverpool look like a team with a huge gap where the star players should be – Luis Suárez now sunning himself in Barcelona, Raheem Sterling settling into life at Manchester City, Philippe Coutinho currently injured and Daniel Sturridge always injured. Without those four, Liverpool are a team seemingly packed full of one-paced midfielders grafting away ahead of a dodgy defence – the complete opposite of the dynamic side created by Claudio Ranieri. As soon as City broke through the red soup in the middle of the pitch, it was 1-0. When Vardy, Mahrez and Okazaki were later isolated against three Liverpool defenders, it was 2-0.

It all looks so simple.

This cannot last forever. Other teams, it is said, will work us out eventually. They will somehow counter our counter-attack and break down our increasingly solid defence. Yet Mark Hughes and Jürgen Klopp both knew what to expect and neither could prevent a comprehensive defeat.

Opposition supporters write on messageboards that it must be incredible to be a Leicester City fan this season. It is. It's also so surreal that it almost feels like living in a parallel universe. We will probably only be able to reflect properly once it has all finished for another year. There's no time to reflect now. On Saturday, it's first against second. A tale of two Cities.

Leicester City 2 (Vardy 2)

Liverpool 0

Team: Schmeichel, Simpson, Morgan, Huth, Fuchs, Mahrez (Ulloa), Drinkwater, Kanté, Albrighton (Gray), Okazaki (King), Vardy

THE VOICE

RIYAD MAHREZ… OVER THE TOP… WILL HE FIND VARDY? YES HE WILL.

Vardy…

Oh yes!

Oh yes!

That's goal of the season!

Jamie Vardy, what a finish!

Over the goalkeeper! Kop end!

It's a goal you would expect a team who are going to win the league to score!

Watch it again, watch it again and watch it again!

That is outrageous! The Liverpool players cannot believe it!

Jamie Vardy, the goal of your life!

Leicester 1 Liverpool 0…

BBC Radio Leicester commentator and lifelong City fan Ian Stringer reflects on the goal that echoed around the world and how it felt to provide the soundtrack.

'I never prepare for what I say when I call a goal,' says Stringer. 'I remember going into the game, I'd done my research as normal. When that ball sat up for him everybody knew what he was going to do. A feeling of euphoria went from my toes up to the top of my head because I knew it was going in.

'I always have to keep a lid on things because of my job and that might surprise some people when I'm screaming the goals in for Leicester City but I remember the heartache at Wembley as a little boy in the early nineties and being distraught as a teenager at Roy Essandoh knocking us out of the FA Cup so when Vardy struck that one, all bets were off and the fan in me was out.'

When the final whistle went, the mayhem began.

'There have been other great goals this season,' says Stringer. 'The Liverpool goal was my first experience of something going viral in the social media age.'

The Premier League used the commentary for their highlights show watched by around 50 million fans worldwide. Another eight million Radio 2 listeners heard it on the Chris Evans show. Radio 1 played it. The New York Times got in touch.

'The organic nature of it is frightening because it just had legs of its own and I was just doing my job. I'm a gob on a stick. But recommendations and endorsements via social media are incredible. If people have done that for me, that's a real blessing.'

Around 100 million people have heard Stringer's commentary of Vardy's wonder strike. This is where professionalism plays a crucial part.

'You've got to keep control of your voice,' he says. 'There are a lot of commentators whose voice can't cope so when they try and go really big, their voice just goes and they sound like a 15-year-old boy again. That's fundamentals like keeping hydrated and keeping a good diet.

'Can you imagine sitting at Wembley as Kenneth Wolstenholme did and England are going to win the World Cup and he's nailed that?' asks Stringer. 'I want to look back on my career and think I've done that. I've got goals wrong but when you've got them right and you hear that people have sought it out, that's really nice.'

It hasn't always been like this. Say the name Troy Deeney to any City fan and it brings back memories of a different kind.

'Deeney was a killer,' says Stringer of the Watford winner in May 2013 that, like so many fans, he found hard to stomach. 'On a professional level though, I got the commentary right. I listened back to that the other day and almost cried. It was horrible. You've got to call the good, the bad and the ugly.'

Thankfully, there have been more good times than bad during Stringer's time at the microphone. Just days before the Deeney goal that caused so much heartache, there was unconfined joy at Anthony Knockaert's last-gasp goal for City in Nottingham.

'I was going for a run a few weeks before the Forest game and just saw in my mind Knockaert scoring an important winner,' says Stringer. 'The crowd love this kid. What would I do? 'Allez Les Bleus' came to me.'

The score is 2-2 at the City Ground on the last day of the season and Forest are pushing for the winner that would propel them into the play-off places. Jeff Schlupp plays the ball forward and Knockaert sets off. He carries the ball deep into opposition territory before giving it to Chris Wood.

'You can see in front of you, with the scoreline as it is, Wood slides it back to him and he's got to score. You've got a split second when you know you've got to call a massive goal and away it went.'

It's in! Anthony Knockaert has done it!

Nottingham has been painted blue!

Anthony Knockaert has scored the goal!

It's the goal!

Allez les bleus! Allez les bleus!

Forest 2 Leicester 3!

'On reflection I think I might have over-egged it a bit with the 'Nottingham has been painted blue' line and gave it the full beans with the Forest season ticket holders in front of me.'

This is the fascinating aspect of Ian Stringer's part in the unfolding Leicester City story. He has to restrain his inner supporter.

'It's a rubbish outlet for my emotion,' he says. 'It's horrendous. A fan takes their nine-year-old boy to watch the game. I can't do that. A fan screams at the full-back when he's having one. I can't do that. A fan can buy a Leicester shirt. Whilst I probably could do that, I'd feel a bit of a clown.'

Speak to Stringer about City for any length of time and there's one topic that gets right to the core of how he's feeling this season.

'What's really hurting me is my nine-year-old son Owen's love of football,' he says. 'He goes to school in Buckinghamshire every day with a Leicester City rucksack. His school's full of Arsenal, Chelsea, Manchester United and Manchester City fans who have always goaded him: 'Who are they? Leicester?' He's dug in last season when we were bottom of the league.

'I see him with his grandad at games, in his Leicester shirt, euphoric and over the moon that his heroes are in front of him on this stage. He can stand there in the playground with his shoulders back and his chest out and say 'I'm a Leicester City fan.'

'I'm living my love for my football club through my nine-year-old boy. I love watching him enjoy the game. I struggle to control my emotions on the air when I think of my children enjoying their football club because Manchester United fans can't feel like this.

'If I have to call a goal that crowns my boyhood team the champions of the Premier League, I pray to the almighty that I don't think about my boy and I don't think about what's happening.'

Stringer is supremely confident that he will be calling that goal.

'I've been through the same washing machine of emotions as every other Leicester City fan but this is different,' he says. 'These players are different. Claudio is different. I think they've got the spirit to do it.

'I'll never complain about my job. I've got one of the best jobs in the world at the minute. I'm a very, very lucky boy.

'It won't ever get as special as this.'

25: MANCHESTER CITY (A)

Saturday 6 February 2016

'LOVELY NORTHERN WEATHER,' SAYS JAMIE VARDY AS HE JOGS out of the tunnel to warm up in relentless, slow drizzle. Riyad Mahrez juggles a ball with his left foot from the away dressing room onto the sodden turf of the Etihad Stadium. Pressure? What pressure? Leicester City are loving life in the big time.

Welcome to the third age of the Premier League.

In the beginning, there was Manchester United and they won the league. Every year. Or so it seemed. Sir Alex Ferguson was their manager and they dominated the landscape of English football.

Then there were Chelsea and Manchester City. Fuelled by the billions of oil magnates, they spent and spent until they were firmly established alongside United in the new order of the Premier League.

Things would never be the same again and supporters of mid-ranking Championship clubs slumped our shoulders as our beloved teams were destined to play out the rest of their days light years away from the pinnacle of the national sport.

Until today.

This afternoon, one of the oil-rich mega-clubs must lower itself to scrapping for every ball, straining for every header and committing to every tackle just to restore parity with a club that has contributed a drop to the vast ocean of Premier League wealth.

Earlier in the week, Manuel Pellegrini announced that he would depart Manchester City in the summer with the Bayern Munich manager Pep Guardiola confirmed as his successor. Outside the ground prior to kick-off, street sellers offer scarves bearing Guardiola's face.

Welcome to Manchester – as a certain billboard once read.

This is our first game of the season to be billed as a clash between title rivals. Win it and we would be six points clear of Manchester City with thirteen games remaining. Lose and the two teams are level on points. No wonder most fans would be happy to zoom back down the M6 with a point.

We know the team these days. The Tinkerman rarely changes it. Schmeichel; Simpson, Morgan, Huth, Fuchs; Mahrez, Drinkwater, Kanté, Albrighton; Vardy, Okazaki.

Two wins in a row, in which five goals were scored and none conceded, have given a whole new complexion to Leicester City's season. In a sense, the hard work has been done. City can afford to lose at both the Etihad and the Emirates and still go on to claim the Premier League trophy, but any sort of result at either ground would be a gigantic bonus. The fans are starting to believe. The media are starting to believe. The players appear to have believed all along.

Kick off.

Our boys are on the front foot straight away. Within the first 60 seconds, N'Golo Kanté has completed a pass, won a header, made an interception and tackled the illustrious Yaya Toure to set his team on an attack that results in a foul on Riyad Mahrez close to the penalty area.

Mahrez delivers the free kick from the right and Robert Huth darts in front of his marker, Martin Demichelis, to touch the ball past Joe Hart. The home side have barely touched the ball and it's already in the back of their net. At the other end of the stadium, spread across three tiers as part of a record attendance, we are a blur of limbs.

Ranieri's men don't stop there, sitting back as expected but enjoying the better opportunities. With ten minutes gone, Mahrez lopes across the centre circle and sets the overlapping Danny Drinkwater clear on the left but the angle is tight and Hart deflects the ball behind. Halfway through the first half Kanté nicks the ball from Sergio Agüero and gives it to Mahrez. The Algerian's long pass finds Vardy who beats Nicolas Otamendi for pace and his low cross almost results in a goal for

Shinji Okazaki.

We're so proud of this team. They're going for it.

Manchester City apply pressure. David Silva pokes a shot wide with the help of a Wes Morgan deflection and referee Anthony Taylor turns down a penalty appeal from Pablo Zabaleta, instead giving a free kick inches outside the box, as the home side probe for a leveller.

Indecision in the away end as Taylor blows the half-time whistle. Would you take a draw now? A tricky question. We're six points clear at the top of the Premier League as it stands, winning at the home of the title favourites. Dare we dream of holding this one-goal lead?

Indecision on the pitch too, but only among those in light blue. Again they push forward and again they're caught out by a trademark counter-attack. Albrighton and Kanté combine to outmuscle Zabaleta and Kanté hares off down the left wing.

Remember the days when we thought he was just a holding midfielder? Remember the days when we didn't realise we had signed one of the best midfielders in the world for less than Derby County paid for Bradley Johnson?

Kanté cuts inside past Fernandinho and plays it forward to Mahrez, who hurdles the challenge of Otamendi. In a matter of seconds, Leicester's two Paris-born superstars have outwitted players who cost eleven times more than them.

It's all about split seconds now. That's how long it takes us to realise Mahrez is one-on-one with Demichelis. That's how long it takes Mahrez to throw one foot and then the other into an extravagant step-over and send Demichelis spinning. That's how long it takes Mahrez's shot to flash past Joe Hart into the net.

It's 2-0. It's Mahrez's fifteenth goal of a remarkable season. Leicester City are dismantling one of the most expensive football teams ever constructed.

Pellegrini responds by withdrawing his captain Yaya Toure and the England international Fabian Delph, each humbled by the workrate and skill of the uncapped duo Kanté and Drinkwater.

On an afternoon of eleven magnificent individual performances, Kasper Schmeichel reminds everyone of his importance to the team by reacting brilliantly to push away a close-range effort from substitute Fernando and the Manchester City players begin to look as though they know it's not their day.

It's City's day and, in particular, it's Robert Huth's day. The big German bashes a header past Hart from a pinpoint Christian Fuchs corner to make it 3-0 after an hour and it's game over.

Agüero heads a late consolation and a Danny Simpson error almost results in a second Agüero goal. Simpson grins at his error, a clear sign this team is simply enjoying its football. No pressure. Six points clear at the top of the Premier League, but no pressure.

The Manchester City fans clap the former Manchester United player Simpson and his team-mates off the pitch at the end of the match and they clap us out of the away end too. Despite all the money and the marketing gloss, this club has known failure and frustration. These fans appreciate effort, commitment and the unfolding of a fairy tale.

We stumble from the away end in a daze. Let it sink in. It won't always be like this.

Later on Saturday, Tottenham win 1-0 at home to Watford. On Sunday, Arsenal win 2-0 at Bournemouth. The gap from the leaders to the two north London sides locked together is five points. Manchester City slip to fourth. Fifth-placed Manchester United, now realistically the only side with faint hopes of replacing City in the Champions League places, concede an injury-time goal to draw 1-1 at Stamford Bridge.

Claudio Ranieri laughs off the news that his side have been installed as the new favourites to win the Premier League. The odds were 5,000/1 before the season began. Now they are 7/4.

Everyone is talking about Leicester City, even England's new rugby union coach Eddie Jones ahead of his side's Six Nations clash with Italy.

'How are Leicester City top of the Premier League?' says Jones. 'It's all because of attitude and how hard they work for each other. It's because the sum of that team is greater than the individuals.'

Ninety minutes in Manchester changed everything.

When Anthony Taylor blew the final whistle at the Etihad Stadium, it only meant three more points - the same as we got for beating Sunderland at home on the opening day or a dishevelled and disinterested Newcastle United at St James' Park in November. However, the nature of the victory, the magnitude of the game, the millions watching worldwide, the confidence of the performance and the lack of precedents meant it only took an hour and a half under a grey northern sky for Leicester City's global profile to go stratospheric.

It's tough for footballers, managers, coaches and especially scouts at other clubs. While on the one hand City's success has allowed fans across the country to dream of their side breaking into the elite, it also leaves no hiding place.

They ask difficult questions: why isn't their club signing players like that? Why aren't they able to keep clean sheets and score at will? Why aren't they getting value for money in the transfer market? Most glaringly, if Okazaki and Kanté and Vardy and Albrighton can run themselves into the ground, why can't their players?

We don't have to worry about our players failing to put in the hard yards in the final third of the season. The concern is instead that the pressure will get to them and that it will be tough for Jamie Vardy not to tense up when a vital chance falls to him in the dying moments or that an increasingly expectant home crowd will grow nervous when City are unable to break down a relegation-threatened team deep into the second half.

There are also mounting comparisons with Diego Simeone's La Liga-winning Atlético Madrid of 2014, a compact, counter-attacking side packed with players who worked for each other. These comparisons could have been made after City's 3-0 wins at Newcastle and Swansea before Christmas when the first signs of a fully-functioning winning machine were apparent. The sense that it would all come crashing down when City came up against 'the big rocks' nagged away though and journalists held off until it was no longer possible to ignore what might happen.

Maybe it takes a Roman to be truly romantic. None of the column inches written about Leicester City this week can match the poetry of Claudio Ranieri's interview with Corriere della Sera: 'I always tell my players to find the fire within themselves. A chance like this will never come round again. Seek that fire, don't be ashamed of it. And they are not ashamed; if anything they demand to dream.'

Don't we all?

Manchester City 1 (Agüero)
Leicester City 3 (Huth 2, Mahrez)
Team: Schmeichel, Simpson, Morgan, Huth, Fuchs, Mahrez (Gray),
Drinkwater, Kanté, Albrighton (Dyer), Okazaki (Ulloa), Vardy

THE NEW YORKER

JASON BECKER IS 33 YEARS OLD. HE WAS BORN AND RAISED IN New York. He lives in Manhattan. And he has supported Leicester City since 1998.

'Fox Soccer started showing a weekly Premier League wrap-up with extended highlights of one game, a bit like Match of the Day,' says Jason. 'The first game we watched was Leicester, featuring American Kasey Keller, against Manchester United. My brother Jordan liked the way they played and decided he would stick with them, and over time I became a bigger and bigger fan as well.

'When we first started following Leicester, we relied on that wrap up show, and caught a couple of games on pay-per-view. Once we were able to find bars with

Setanta subscriptions, and lax ID checkers, we would try to catch whatever games we could, though they were few and far between.'

Jason and Jordan decided to form a supporters' group to make it easier for followers in New York to connect with other City fans and find out where to watch their club.

'Ever since we've been back in the Premier League, it's been incredibly easy to watch games over here,' says Jason. 'This might make the folks in Leicester a bit jealous, but we can watch every single Premier League game live, even when travelling to other parts of the country. The coverage is fantastic, and we can also watch HD streams from NBC on our mobile devices.'

As excellent as the coverage is, it can't beat the real thing. Jason made his first trip to see City play in February. He was hoping for a better experience than Jordan, whose only visit to date remains a defeat to Preston North End in the season City were relegated to League One – not quite the same as seeing Ranieri's men take on Liverpool and Manchester City.

'We have a pretty good idea of what the atmosphere is like at the King Power from the television but I still wasn't quite prepared for what it was like that Tuesday night for the Liverpool game,' says Jason. 'The intensity in the stadium was incredible. I felt it as soon as I pushed through the turnstiles. I was blown away by the noise in the ground, and when Vardy hit that wonder strike, everyone and everything erupted. I felt a wave of belief rush around the stadium and I think that was the moment when a lot of fans realised that this club could really do the unthinkable.

'The atmosphere at the Etihad was much flatter. To be fair, Robert Huth could take a lot of credit for quietening the home fans after scoring three minutes in. The away end was still a blast, though. I bumped into some folks that I'd watched a match with back in NYC and had a great time standing and singing with them in Manchester.'

Jason's trip was improved even further by the club's welcome. He was treated to a tour of the ground and invited onto the pitch before the Liverpool game to meet Alan Birchenall. It was to get even better once the second game had finished.

'The day after the Manchester City game the club arranged for me to spend some time hanging out with Christian Fuchs, who has family connections in NYC,' he says. 'He's just like what a lot of fans probably think he's like based on his interviews and social media posts. It's all genuine. There are some really good guys on this team; they're a great bunch to root for.

'My brothers and I have always felt a close connection to the club. We've met tons of fans from Leicester while watching games together in NYC, and they've always been great to us. My trip to Leicester only confirmed that feeling and I was blown away by how incredibly well the entire city treated me.

'I really feel like the people of Leicester deserve this success.'

26: ARSENAL (A)

Sunday 14 February 2016

THE DEFINITIVE ACCOUNT OF LIFE AS A FOOTBALL FAN IS arguably Fever Pitch, Nick Hornby's autobiographical book about Arsenal's 1989 First Division title triumph sealed in the final moments of a dramatic win at Anfield. In 1997, it was made into a film. The closing scenes portray Arsenal fans dancing around the streets of north London clad in red and white. Imagine being a Tottenham fan in the midst of such delirium. Imagine being a Liverpool fan.

Leicester City are unchanged for the trip to the Emirates Stadium, meaning Ranieri keeps the same team for a sixth league game in a row – the first time this season for any Premier League club. So once again it's Schmeichel; Simpson, Morgan, Huth, Fuchs; Mahrez, Kanté, Drinkwater, Albrighton; Okazaki and Vardy who are charged with bringing three points back to the east Midlands.

Arsène Wenger's side are returning to full strength following a typical Arsenal mid-season injury crisis. Key players, most notably Alexis Sánchez and Francis Coquelin, are back in the starting eleven. It's a formidable line up on paper, but so was Manchester City's.

The pattern of the game is entirely predictable. Arsenal control possession and probe for an opening. City sit deep and wait to spring the feared counter-attack. As in so many games this season, Ranieri's men make excellent chances from little possession. The best opportunity sees Jamie Vardy leap high above Hector Béllerín to send a header on goal which is saved low to his right by Petr Čech.

Half time beckons when the game takes the first of many twists. Inevitably, it comes from a City counter. N'Golo Kanté, magnificent throughout the first half, bursts down the right wing and manages to shift the ball forward despite being taken out by Laurent Koscielny. Vardy takes up possession and moves into the area. His touch is poor, leading Arsenal's left-back Nacho Monreal to momentarily believe he can steal the ball. Monreal dangles a leg and Vardy is sent tumbling. Penalty.

Vardy, entrusted with the spot kick following Riyad Mahrez's missed efforts against Bournemouth and Aston Villa, smashes the ball into the corner of the net and we celebrate wildly at the opposite end of the stadium.

Referee Martin Atkinson blows the half time whistle. As it stands, we are – whisper it – eight points clear at the top of the Premier League table.

Things can only get worse. The atmosphere becomes toxic. Is Atkinson strong enough to ignore the shrieks of indignation from the home fans?

At the start of the second half, Danny Simpson commits two soft fouls in the space of a few minutes and is shown yellow cards on both occasions, swiftly followed by a red – City's first of the season. The waves of red and white attacks begin.

Ranieri responds by bringing off Mahrez, the star creator, to introduce Marcin Wasilewski. We park the bus. Shinji Okazaki is soon sacrificed in favour of Demarai Gray, leaving Vardy to form a lonely front line of one. Now the bus is a double decker.

Arsenal pour forward and create numerous overlaps, especially on their left with the combination of Monreal and Sánchez, but City are holding firm. Indeed, it takes the home side 70 minutes to force their first shot on target. When it happens, Kasper Schmeichel is left exposed and the scores are level: Olivier Giroud flicks a clever header into the path of substitute Theo Walcott who beats City's Danish goalkeeper from close range.

The clock on the big screen at the Emirates Stadium counts down rather than up. It's agonising. Arsenal waste chance after chance with Schmeichel pulling off one spectacular save from Giroud at full stretch while Per Mertesacker unfathomably glances a header wide from inside the six-yard box. City are so close to a vital point. So very close.

Time is ticking towards the end of four minutes of stoppage time when Monreal goes up to head a loose ball and Wasilewski pole-axes him with a senselessly robust challenge. Referee Atkinson blows for a foul and we all know what will happen. Mesut Özil floats the ball into the area. For the second time, an Arsenal substitute finds the net. This time it's Danny Welbeck, returning from a lengthy injury absence. The stadium erupts. All of City's efforts are in vain.

2-1 to Arsenal: an identical scoreline to the same fixture last season but the circumstances could hardly be more different. That night, City remained bottom of the league after defeat. This time, we remain top. Back then, we went in at half-time two goals down and rallied with Andrej Kramarić missing a glorious chance to equalise. It felt as morale-boosting as a defeat can be. City were behind in the game for over an hour. We were behind for just over a minute this time, but it feels a hundred times worse.

In fact, it feels worse than any defeat last season. Football supporters aren't the best at retaining perspective in the heat of the moment. This is gut-wrenching, pit-of-the-stomach anguish we hadn't previously felt all season. It's painful. What if Simpson hadn't been sent off? What if Wasilewski hadn't made that challenge? What if Welbeck had sent his header wide? Immediately following the final whistle, it feels as though we will reflect upon this moment as crucial to the outcome of the title race.

The Arsenal players and fans certainly seem to think so. The players complete a lap of honour before retreating to the dressing room to take a group photo. Outside, we're watching a re-enactment of Fever Pitch. They're hugging each other. Dancing. Skipping down the street. On the way up to Finsbury Park tube station, Arsenal songs echo around the houses.

They are less happy a few hours later when their rivals Tottenham Hotspur record an impressive win at the Etihad Stadium to move onto 51 points, level with Arsenal.

There are twelve games left but two weeks until the next one. We remain two points clear of both north London clubs and six points above Manchester City. Ranieri grants his players the first week of the fortnight off in recognition of their efforts in the past few games.

When we last lost to Arsenal, a subsequent win over Norwich City was the first of a ten-game unbeaten run. Again it's the Canaries up next. A similar sequence of results would surely bring a first ever top flight title to Leicester. The nature of defeat at the Emirates can only strengthen the resolve.

Arsenal 2 (Walcott, Welbeck)

Leicester City 1 (Vardy)

Team: Schmeichel, Simpson, Morgan, Huth, Fuchs, Mahrez (Wasilewski), Drinkwater, Kanté, Albrighton (King), Okazaki (Gray), Vardy

THE SWITCH

'FUCHS IS IN. EXPECTED THAT. SCHLUPP UP TO LEFT WING. RIYAD
on the bench. That's a surprise...

'Hang on... Simpson?'

So went the conversations on the way down the hill from the council car park to
Carrow Road on an unseasonably sunny day in early October.

We were quite enjoying Leicester City's new reputation as devil-may-care cavaliers of the Premier League. We loved watching our team storm forward in numbers
and devastate the opposition on the counter. The only problem was the sieve-like
defence at the other end of the pitch. The previous weekend at the end of September, Arsenal struck five past Kasper Schmeichel.

For the visit to Norwich City, Claudio Ranieri brought in Danny Simpson. Was
this the answer? It was certainly something different - the attack-minded Ritchie De
Laet replaced at right-back by a capable defender but not a man to overlap to great
effect.

It seemed that Ranieri was aping Nigel Pearson's tendency to retreat into defensive mode when problems arose. Plan B meant back to basics.

The thing is: it worked.

The switch to Simpson and Fuchs helped to shore up a porous back line and
the defensive record went from nine goals conceded in three games to nine in nine.

As the season went on, there were even glimpses of improved attacking play from
City's new first-choice right back and Ranieri saw fit to let De Laet move out on loan
to Championship promotion hopefuls Middlesbrough.

Simpson's raid forward at former club Newcastle United in November led to a
scruffy Shinji Okazaki goal. He frequently found himself in an advanced position
towards the end of matches, helping to close games out with impressive one-touch
passing.

So it was with a certain reluctance that Simpson trudged from the pitch at the
Emirates Stadium, knowing that his team-mates would have to work doubly hard
in the remaining minutes. In the end, the very end, it was the man who replaced
him at right-back, Marcin Wasilewski, whose robust challenge led to a heartbreaking
Arsenal winner.

Wasilewski displayed a rashness that we hadn't seen all season from Simpson. The
right-back role has been Simpson's own - surely one of the most unlikely members
of a title-chasing side in Premier League history.

In a team far surpassing expectations, Simpson is a contender to be recognised as the most improved of all. Nobody could have foreseen it, especially last summer when an assault conviction threatened Simpson's presence at the club. He carried out his community service calling numbers in a bingo hall.

Now City must cope against Norwich without one of their most dependable performers and supporters worry about the impact his loss will have on such a settled side.

'Hang on… no Simpson…'

27: NORWICH CITY (H)

Saturday 27 February 2016

NORWICH CITY SIT OUTSIDE THE RELEGATION ZONE ON GOAL difference, conceding 21 times in the seven games since they last won. They had lost six in a row in all competitions before going 2-0 up at home to West Ham United, conceding twice and nearly conceding again. They have only won twice away in the league all season and none of their players have managed five league goals.

This is a game title-chasing Leicester City cannot afford to lose. It may also act as a reminder that nothing has been achieved yet. We had fewer points than Norwich's current total at this stage of the previous season. It was then City who were able to benefit from others taking three points for granted against eleven men who fought for ninety minutes.

We've been waiting two weeks for this since the heartbreak of the Emirates so let's fast forward through a deeply frustrating encounter to the closing minutes of the game. The score is still 0-0. The best efforts – a free header inside the six-yard box from a corner and a 25-yard drive that flew away from the goalkeeper and just past the post – have come from the away side.

Claudio Ranieri has gambled and thrown on an extra striker, Leonardo Ulloa, in place of debutant right-back Daniel Amartey. City go to three at the back: Marc Albrighton is shifted to right wing-back, Riyad Mahrez is moved into the number ten role and Ulloa joins Jamie Vardy in attack.

Alex Tettey, Norwich's midfield enforcer, has pushed up from his position, leaving an unguarded defence. Drinkwater turns away from Tettey and finds Mahrez in an ocean of space in front of Norwich's back line. Mahrez carries the ball forward unopposed. Two Norwich defenders back off, wary of the Algerian's trickery.

Little wonder. Earlier in the game, a simple drop of the shoulder turned two of them inside out. Mahrez made the wrong decision on that occasion, opting to shoot and finding his attempt blocked. Now, as we head towards injury time, he resists the urge and instead slips a pass to Albrighton down the right.

Albrighton drives in a low, hard cross. Norwich goalkeeper John Ruddy can't reach it. His defenders don't want to risk sticking out a leg and conceding an own goal. Vardy slides in but can only get the faintest of touches.

Ranieri's tactical gamble pays off. Mahrez found the space in a central area. Albrighton raided forward from a deeper position. Vardy can't convert but his touch takes the ball away from Ryan Bennett, one of three Norwich centre-backs, and lands right in Ulloa's path.

Ulloa sticks it away. Sliding in, with his weaker left foot, he sticks it away and City have won the game with just minutes remaining. The King Power Stadium had been relatively quiet, supporters newly accustomed to brilliance left nervy as a prime opportunity to secure three points faded. Ulloa's goal changes that in an instant. The scenes are reminiscent of those we endured at the Emirates a fortnight earlier. That late goal cost City a point and felt like a disaster. This one gains two and causes an earthquake, or at least a tremor recorded by a group of local primary school children as part of a science experiment.

This is a reminder of the true agony and ecstasy of a title challenge and it doesn't stop with the final whistle that sounds minutes after Ulloa's intervention. We aren't just gripped by one match each weekend as their side fights for an unlikely league title – we're also captivated by those of our nearest rivals.

Tottenham and Arsenal kick off simultaneously on Sunday afternoon, each aiming to close the five-point gap created by City's late win. Tottenham fall behind in the first half to a struggling Swansea side at White Hart Lane, while Arsenal concede two goals to Manchester United's newest hero, the 18-year-old striker Marcus Rashford, at Old Trafford. The Premier League trophy has never seemed as close as this. There's a siege in north London though, which ends with two second-half goals for Tottenham and a 2-1 win that takes Mauricio Pochettino's side back to within two points of the top.

Pochettino's men are out on their own in second place. Arsenal fail to force their way back into the game against a youthful Manchester United side decimated by injury. It finishes 3-2 to United and an inquest begins. City will face pressure between now and the end of the season but our players and manager won't have to put up with anything like the fury Arsenal's fans launch at their team's weak display. The supporters who danced in the street at Danny Welbeck's last-gasp winner now appear to have given up.

This is no time to be giving anything up. Thankfully, Leonardo didn't.

Leicester City 1 (Ulloa)

Norwich City 0

Team: Schmeichel, Amartey (Ulloa), Morgan, Huth, Fuchs, Mahrez, Drinkwater, Kanté (King), Albrighton, Okazaki (Schlupp), Vardy

THE KING

ANDY KING HAS PLAYED FOR LEICESTER CITY IN LEAGUE ONE and the Johnstone's Paint Trophy. He's played for Leicester City in the Championship and the League Cup. He's played for Leicester City in the Premier League and the FA Cup. He might, just might, play for Leicester City in the Champions League.

What a story. What a man.

We love Kingy. He's been there with us through it all. His mum and dad have been there too, in away ends up and down the country. We love him almost as much as they do.

King scored eight goals in 21 games as City's Under 18s won the Premier League at Academy level in 2007. He was given his debut by Gary Megson later that year and scored his first goal under Ian Holloway two months later, but finally found the manager he, and the club, had been looking for when Nigel Pearson was appointed in the summer of 2008.

Pearson watched as a young reserve side scored eight against local non-league side Quorn in a pre-season friendly and noted one delicious lobbed finish from a tall, skinny central midfielder. When City's first-ever league campaign in the third tier kicked off, Andy King was in the team.

He stayed in the team and he scored goals – lots of them. He even kept scoring despite Pearson's departure, becoming a figurehead for the club when Sven-Göran Eriksson made him captain at the age of 22.

Then the goals dried up, the captaincy was moved on and King settled into a new role during Pearson's second spell, playing deeper in midfield and concentrating more on his defensive duties.

New players have been brought in over the years to compete for King's place in midfield – Danny Drinkwater, Matty James, Esteban Cambiasso, N'Golo Kanté – but he has remained reliable when called upon.

In an age in which so many footballers seem obsessed with angling for transfers, it has been refreshing to see King stay loyal to City. He could have agitated for a move when he was seen as one of the best players outside the Premier League. He could have handed in a transfer request once he was usurped from the starting eleven. Instead, he has stayed and reaped the rewards – success with club and country.

The visit of West Bromwich Albion offers a rare opportunity for Andy King to start a Premier League game. We yearn for a reminder of the past: to see him ghost into the box like he did years ago and slot a finish into the corner of the net.

St David's Day. The Welsh international returns to the fold. The scene is set.

28: WEST BROMWICH ALBION (H)

Tuesday 1 March 2016

FEBRUARY IS GONE AND CITY ARE ON THE MARCH. ELEVEN games to go. Eleven men charged with bringing glory to their football club. Claudio Ranieri makes two changes to his side as City face another bottom-half team at home just three days on from the late, late show against Norwich. Danny Simpson returns from suspension at right-back in place of Daniel Amartey, while Andy King replaces the injured N'Golo Kanté.

Since the arrival of Tony Pulis, West Bromwich Albion have taken over from his previous club Stoke City as the least attractive footballing side in the Premier League. It's hard to be too critical in the current climate though. Hard to look down the nose. So many Tottenham and Arsenal supporters are doing the same to the tactics employed by Claudio Ranieri.

It seems laughable given the unprecedented levels of entertainment served up by the likes of Jamie Vardy and Riyad Mahrez, but City appear to be gaining a reputation among their rivals similar to that associated with Pulis and his teams. Less possession. Fewer short passes. More strong tackles. It appears to add up to a charge sheet for some, with the evidence provided as a backs-to-the-wall win at White Hart

Lane and some robust challenges at the Emirates.

The perfect defence against those accusations duly arrives with a highly entertaining encounter. There were hints Albion would not be as defensive as some suggested. Their previous game saw Salomon Rondon, Saido Berahino and Stephane Sessegnon form a potent three-man attack in a 3-2 win over Crystal Palace. Pulis retains this approach against City.

Rondon, a well-built Venezuelan with an impressive recent goalscoring record in the Spanish and Russian leagues, is an interesting example of the Premier League's pulling power.

It takes a strong man to outmuscle Robert Huth and Rondon is certainly that. The Albion striker gets behind Huth and slots the ball under Kasper Schmeichel to put his side ahead. Ten home league games have been and gone since City last conceded the opening goal. The last time it happened, back in September, Aston Villa went on to lose 3-2. Those were the days of the fightback, when we went two goals down four times in five games and only lost once. The defence has since been strengthened to such a degree that no stirring comebacks have been necessary.

We recognise this is new territory in the context of a title challenge. After the momentary silence comes a wall of noise from the Kop to drown out the visiting supporters.

The nature of support is a hot topic. Later in the evening, thousands of Aston Villa fans will walk out of their home game with Everton in protest at the way their club is being run. Liverpool supporters did the same at a recent game to highlight the issue of ticket prices. It's been less than a fortnight since a coin thrown by a West Bromwich Albion fan struck one of his own players, Chris Brunt, in the face after a match.

Amidst all of this, we can only reflect what is happening on the pitch. Our team is giving everything and the least we can do is to match that in the stands. Every attack is accompanied by a huge roar and two of them culminate in wild celebrations. First, Danny Drinkwater fires a shot from outside the box which takes a huge deflection off Albion defender Jonas Olsson and loops up over goalkeeper Ben Foster. Moments before half time, Drinkwater's central midfield partner Andy King sweeps the ball into the net following a brilliant Riyad Mahrez flick to put City into the lead. The players need a rest at half time and so do the fans.

The second half is even more draining. A promising City counter-attack is halted at its earliest stage when Mahrez attempts to break away but handles the ball to concede a free kick on the edge of his own penalty area. Craig Gardner sends it over the wall and into the top corner with Schmeichel unable to react. Again that silence and again that roar.

Like rush-hour traffic brought to a stop by a red light, several glorious chances pass by before referee Mark Clattenburg blows the final whistle. An Okazaki header. A Morgan shot. A Mahrez bicycle kick. Whether it's saved by Foster, crashing against the crossbar or ending up in the crowd, the one place the ball doesn't come to rest is the back of the net.

While one more point is added to the tally, it's easy to see why most fans see it as two points dropped. Even so, we go three points clear at the top of the Premier League ahead of the following night's games. Second-placed Tottenham, winners of six league games in a row, make the short trip to Upton Park for the final time before West Ham move into their new stadium. A win would take Tottenham top for the first time in seven years.

Elsewhere, Arsenal welcome Swansea City to the Emirates Stadium needing to get their title tilt back on track after losing at Old Trafford and fourth-placed Manchester City head to Anfield four days after beating Liverpool in the League Cup final.

Perhaps one of the three will drop precious points. We watch and wait.

West Ham are the first to take the lead with what turns out to be the only goal of the game, a near-post Michail Antonio header from a corner. Tottenham, well below-par in the first half, improve after the break but Harry Kane misses a glorious chance from close range and a raucous Upton Park crowd sees its team home. West Ham move to within one point of the Champions League places.

That proximity is possible because Manchester City crash and burn on Merseyside, conceding three times without reply to a rampant Liverpool side intent on gaining a modicum of revenge for their Wembley defeat.

The best news of the evening comes from the Emirates. That initially seems unlikely when Joel Campbell puts Arsenal ahead but Wayne Routledge draws Swansea level before half time. Arsenal create chances but the woodwork denies Alexis Sánchez twice and Olivier Giroud once. Instead, Swansea lead when Ashley Williams bundles a free kick into the net. Arsenal push forward but, like Tottenham and Manchester City, they lose.

What seems even more crucial than the bare facts of goals, points, wins and losses is the mental ramifications. Sánchez is quoted as having said before his side's defeat to Manchester United that: 'we lack hunger to believe that we can be champions.'

His manager is similarly reflective. 'I am worrying about our results,' says Arsène Wenger after the Swansea game. 'We don't dream. We have to be realistic and come back to what we do well – the basics.'

It's a sensational, pinch-yourself night for Claudio Ranieri, his players and all supporters. City remain three points clear of Tottenham and six ahead of Arsenal. The next Premier League match pits the north London rivals against each other and the stakes could hardly be higher.

Wednesday morning's papers focused on City supposedly throwing away the initiative. 24 hours later, it's apparently our title to lose. There is revisionism too, as the succession of chances missed during an agonising last half hour against West Bromwich Albion is suddenly re-imagined by the media as evidence of a team with unrivalled belief and desire.

It's a day late but it's true. Nobody wants this more than Leicester City.

Leicester City 2 (Olsson og, King)
West Bromwich Albion 2 (Rondon, Gardner)
Team: Schmeichel, Simpson, Morgan, Huth, Fuchs (Gray), Mahrez,
Drinkwater, King, Albrighton (Schlupp), Okazaki (Ulloa), Vardy

THE SAMURAI

IN AN INTERVIEW WITH THE JAPANESE SPORTS MAGAZINE *Number*, Shinji Okazaki recalled a training session shortly before Christmas when he met a low, hard cross at the near post with a superb diving header into the net.

The other players raced up to him saying 'Wow – didn't know you could do that!' The truth is that he had already scored exactly that type of goal in a pre-season friendly at Birmingham before the Premier League season had even started.

As the season wore on, we began to wonder whether Okazaki was sacrificing his main strengths for the team. Perhaps he was too timid to assert his authority on a squad full of strong personalities.

An incident during the home game with Stoke in January showed that Okazaki was finally finding his voice. Riyad Mahrez played a ball through, but Okazaki couldn't get on the end of it. Mahrez had a go at him.

'Your pass was too weak!' Okazaki shouted back.

We were beginning to see the real Shinji Okazaki – the one who had threatened to take the Premier League by storm in two impressive showings to start the season.

Ken Harvey, a City fan who has lived in Japan for nearly fifteen years, offers a fascinating insight into the effect Okazaki has had on the club's global profile.

'Mauricio Pochettino started it all for me during the 2002 World Cup,' says Harvey. 'He tripped Michael Owen in Sapporo, England beat Argentina 1-0 and the whole experience was so wonderful that I decided to move here permanently. Before the game I'd spent several days walking around the city with a sign reading 'I Need a Ticket', feeling very nervous as I had no idea about Japanese laws on buying and selling tickets.

'I remembered this when I came back to the UK for the 2-2 draw with West Brom. Outside the ground I saw two young Japanese guys with a sign reading 'I Need a Ticket'. I walked over to chat, but I was beaten to it by a steward, who was giving them a good talking to.

'The Japanese guys clearly didn't understand a word, and I offered to interpret. 'Tell them they'll be arrested if they don't stop', the steward said. I said to the Japanese guys words to the effect of 'Listen, this jobsworth wants you to stop, but let's ignore him. Put the sign away and I'll meet you round the corner in five minutes and help you find a ticket.' I turned back to the steward, who thanked me.'

The Japanese supporters had flown in on one of the increasingly popular Premier League package tours. They had tickets for a game at Stoke the following night, but were understandably keen to see Okazaki while they were in England.

'Shinji was so good that night, buzzing about all over the place,' says Harvey, who can understand the time Okazaki took to settle properly in his new surroundings.

'I've had my own problems with cultural differences since I've been in Japan,' he says. 'I often used to stand in the crazy corner at Filbert Street because you could let it all hang out. The shouting, the screaming, the constant stream of expletives and Italian-style gestures. But this kind of behaviour is not looked upon fondly here – especially by your neighbours at 1am in the morning through the wafer thin walls of an average Japanese apartment.

'The equivalent of Sky here shows five Premier League games live every week. It's always obvious which games they will choose – the big five. But this season, with Okazaki in the team, every Leicester game has been live. The problem is the time difference – they typically kick off way past the time people are expected to tip-toe around the room, listen to music on headphones and generally keep things silent so as not to cause a disturbance.

'I usually watch the games at my partner's flat, and she had got a letter from her landlord the week before the game at Manchester City complaining about the noise. I knew this was my fault. It's easy to turn the TV down, but it's not so easy to stop the involuntary screams that naturally accompany this miraculous season.

'For the Manchester City game, though, I knew I had to put a lid on it. My partner was telling me she might have to move out if the problems continued. So of course we go and produce the finest display in our history. It was like having a ticket in the wrong end – trying to hold everything inside.

'Huth's early goal was okay, but it was two second half moments that did for me. When Mahrez danced through their defence and pulled that shot past Joe Hart, out came a raw yelp of joy. And when Danny Simpson put that back pass at Agüero's feet, out came a scream of pure horror.

'My partner is still in the same flat, but the climax of the season is still to come, so the neighbours ain't heard nothing yet.'

Prepare the property listings. Leicester City are gearing up for a title run-in.

29: WATFORD (A)

Saturday 5 March 2016

WELCOME TO VICARAGE ROAD – THE SCENE OF LEICESTER CITY'S heartbreaking play-off semi-final defeat in 2013 and redemptive 3-0 league victory later that year, a memorable win on the way to a title. Now we're back. Can the story be repeated?

Before we can find out, what is billed as the biggest north London derby of all time takes place between Tottenham Hotspur and Arsenal at White Hart Lane.

The home crowd are understandably expectant. Arsenal are imploding under the pressure of trying to win a league title supposedly earmarked for them. Now their nearest neighbours and greatest rivals are ready to snatch it from them. With the storyline firmly set, the fly in the ointment is Leicester City. How can it be the most important game ever played between two of English football's most famous old names if neither go on to win anything this season?

Still, Tottenham can go top with victory and even those not given to hyperbole must concede this is a crucial encounter.

Arsenal strike first when Aaron Ramsey cleverly flicks the ball past Hugo Lloris and they hold the lead until the break. This time it's the defensive midfielder Francis

Coquelin who presses Arsenal's well-worn self-destruct button when he slides in on Harry Kane. Second yellow. Red card. Ten men. The noise cranks up and the team in red folds. Toby Alderweireld equalises on the hour and Harry Kane curls a brilliant second just moments later.

If Tottenham can see out the remaining half hour against their despondent rivals, a first league title since 1961 could be well within reach.

But they can't. Tottenham are top of the league table for thirteen minutes before Alexis Sánchez strikes to put Arsenal level and City back at the summit. It finishes two apiece and the reaction from both sets of players at the final whistle is telling. Neither team celebrates, but we do.

The three o'clock kick-offs come and go with a routine victory for Manchester City over Aston Villa, the team that everyone throws around like a rag doll for ninety minutes. Clocks tick down and 5.30pm approaches.

A pink glow frames the Rookery Stand as the sun sets, adding to the surreal feel. Leicester City can go five points clear at the top of the Premier League with nine games remaining.

Vicarage Road is not the most intimidating football stadium. The words to the chorus of 'Your Song' by Elton John are emblazoned across the back of one stand. A man dressed as a seven-foot hornet dances in front of the away end. Throughout the game, the faint sound of tribal drums can be heard as though the game is taking place in a tropical rainforest. The pink glow fades and the game begins.

Troy Deeney and Odion Ighalo, Watford's fearsome front pairing, are off-form and, in any case, our centre-backs are well-equipped to deal with them. Deeney and Ighalo have outmuscled defenders all season, scoring 22 goals in total. Wes Morgan and Robert Huth flex their biceps and prepare for battle.

Watford are a good side. They work hard and they play attractive football. There are shades of this City side about them but they lack creativity. The visitors make the better chances but the scores remain goalless at half time with Deeney and Jamie Vardy missing the best opportunities at each end.

Ranieri shuffles his pack at the break, taking off Shinji Okazaki and Marc Albrighton. On come Andy King and Jeff Schlupp, two Academy graduates charged with turning one point into all three.

The game needs something special. Slowly, City begin to turn the screw following another masterful tactical change from Ranieri. King slots into midfield and Danny Drinkwater drops behind to dictate the play. Riyad Mahrez has greater licence to roam off his wing to find gaps in front of the Watford defence.

Eleven minutes into the second half, neat interplay in midfield results in King sliding a pass into space down the left for Christian Fuchs. The left-back advances unopposed and swings a cross into the box. The ball is headed clear by Watford's makeshift centre-back Nathan Aké but it drops straight to Mahrez, who has hung back cleverly on the edge of the area. Mahrez shapes to hit the ball first time and instead takes a touch.

From the away end, we can just about see the ball beyond the goalkeeper and two Watford defenders. It's up to Riyad Mahrez to find a way past all three. He strikes with power and precision and Heurelho Gomes is beaten. The away end erupts and the celebration is longer and louder than most. Given the way our side has defended recently, we feel confident that all three points have been secured.

Ranieri's men are at their irresistible, counter-attacking best for the next ten minutes. Schlupp, Vardy and Mahrez form a rapid front three and Watford are clinging on. The travelling City support responds with the best away end of the season so far: non-stop singing at top volume.

Watford force a couple of chances. Nordin Amrabat, booked in the first half for diving, stays on his feet under a challenge from Fuchs and fires the ball into Schmeichel's midriff. Later, Ighalo's header from close range is again directed straight at the City goalkeeper.

There's a late scare when Mahrez pulls up holding the back of his knee. A collective intake of breath from those behind the goal. A nervous few minutes. City's match-winner manages to continue before being replaced by Daniel Amartey. It's not a hamstring injury. It's just cramp. Purest relief.

Mahrez supplied the magic but the star man is Danny Drinkwater, controlling the game from midfield on his 26th birthday against a team he once represented on loan. Drinkwater is one of six players to have played in the play-off nightmare three years earlier. Of that list, the other starters – Schmeichel, Morgan and Vardy – have been among the best players in the country this season. The remaining two – King and Schlupp – have had to play supporting roles for various reasons but both have been central to tonight's crucial victory.

The end of the game brings another celebration longer and louder than most to greet final whistles. There have been so many memorable moments in this unfathomable season and this is yet another. Ranieri's name is sung but the Italian points at his players, telling us to send the credit in their direction instead. Fists clenched, the players walk towards the away end and the fans respond. Songs stop and a roar goes up, reminiscent of an afternoon towards the end of the previous season when Nigel Pearson roused the City fans at Turf Moor following another hard-fought 1-0 win.

It's getting real now. It's getting serious. City are five points clear with nine games to go. Those who backed them to win the league, whether in hope, jest or expectation, are starting to cash out. One punter takes £29,000. Another takes £71,000. Yet more are letting their wagers ride amid building belief that this is actually happening. Leicester City are favourites to win the Premier League.

Watford 0

Leicester City 1 (Mahrez)

Team: Schmeichel, Simpson, Morgan, Huth, Fuchs, Mahrez (Amartey), Drinkwater, Kanté, Albrighton (Schlupp), Okazaki (King), Vardy

THE BOARDROOM

'ALL THESE ONE-NILS ARE AGONY,' SAYS JON HOLMES, A leading football agent and lifelong Leicester City fan. 'I was watching the Watford game on television and I was a bloody nervous wreck.'

Holmes was briefly chairman of the club in the eventful 2002/03 season that saw administration, the threat of liquidation and eventual promotion.

He gives a brief appraisal of Vichai and Aiyawatt Srivaddhanaprabha, the father and son whose millions have helped transform Leicester City from Championship also-rans into Premier League title contenders.

'They've bunged a load of money in and you can't knock it.'

There have been more glowing tributes to the Srivaddhanaprabhas, who spent £39million to purchase Leicester City in 2010 and have invested over £100million in total in improving every aspect of the club, but Holmes tells it as he sees it.

'Nobody much from outside the club has had any football dealings with the owners,' he says. 'They keep themselves to themselves. Susan Whelan's a very capable chief executive even though she knew three parts of nothing about football when she arrived.'

The decision to replace Nigel Pearson with Claudio Ranieri was initially met with scepticism from large sections of the City support.

Shortly after Ranieri's appointment, Whelan told the assembled media: 'We don't talk about our business in the public domain every day. I am confident and sure the majority of the fans will have trusted in the judgement of the board.

'Claudio is a man of vast experience and knowledge. We are very pleased to have him here at the club and he is going to lead us into the next chapter of the club's history.

'We are very proud to have him.'

The decision has proven to be perfect but Holmes believes the process that led to Ranieri's arrival was unnecessarily lengthy.

'The owners have twice got rid of managers without any clear idea of who would replace them,' he says. 'Martin George [City chairman in the mid-1990s] always said to me you need to have two in reserve because your manager could lose eight on the trot or he could get poached.

'You need to have that backup plan. Twice they haven't and twice they've got away with it. With Ranieri, suddenly they hit the jackpot.

'A lot of successful people don't know how lucky they are.'

Holmes's experience in the Leicester City boardroom was very different. In 2002, he formed a consortium to help a club in crisis.

Andrew Taylor, a shareholder who later joined the board, reflects on a time of great upheaval:

'The events leading up to administration formed a financial 'perfect storm'. The club had been relegated from the Premier League in the 2001/02 season, the new stadium had been built and needed funding and the collapse of ITV Digital eliminated a potentially lucrative income stream for clubs relegated from the Premier League.

'Playing contracts didn't have clauses cutting wages in the event of relegation so the wage bill was disproportionately high for the club's revenue. Thankfully, there were no point deductions and no desperate need to sell players in those days.'

When Holmes was told the club would be going into administration, he put together the consortium that would save City. His long-term friend and client Gary Lineker was brought on board as the figurehead and Holmes was invited to become chairman.

'I didn't want to do it,' he says. 'Eventually I said I'd do it for the rest of the season. I found it a pain in the arse being chairman. If I'd been older, less ambitious business-wise and had more control, I might have done it for longer.

'It was a struggle to raise the money. We just about got there.'

The consortium led by Holmes and Lineker eventually took control in February 2003. One of its members, James Johnson, a lawyer who has supported City since 1970, became a director.

'The club actually came close to going out of business completely,' says Johnson. 'Most supporters believed the club was saved when the consortium was named as the preferred bidder before Christmas. In fact, no deal was done at that point and for a few hours early in January it looked like Leicester City would disappear forever.'

'The club is light years away now from where it was in the post-administration period,' says Taylor. 'Football finance in the Football League is not for the fainthearted. For those clubs without wealthy backers a typical start to the season assumes reasonably high cash reserves from selling season tickets.

'By January, when fans were hoping the club would be active in the transfer window, the cash would have dwindled to the point that the club was operating in its overdraft, then capped at £2million. So it was a very precarious hand-to-mouth existence which meant a need for short term initiatives to generate cash, like early bird discounts for season ticket purchases or the sale of better players to build up the cash balance and reduce the wage bill of the playing staff.'

'The gulf between the Premier League and the Football League was huge and it's getting bigger still given the new media deal that takes effect from next season.'

In 2006/07, the first season after parachute payments ceased, the annual players' wage bill stood at £5million and the club's income from Football League sponsorship was less than £2million.

In February 2016, there were media reports that Jamie Vardy's new contract would cost City over £4million per year – an investment made possible in large part by the Premier League's 2014/15 payment to the club of £71.6million.

The numbers are staggering to the average fan but the Srivaddhanaprabhas have often gone above and beyond in their quest for success, acknowledging the importance of maintaining good relations with the club's fan base.

'They have shown remarkable generosity of spirit in the free scarves, T-shirts, food and drink they have provided for supporters,' says Johnson. 'They have also respected the traditions of our club. We still play in blue. We still come out to the Post Horn Gallop. They could have tried to change that.'

These days, Taylor, Johnson and Holmes are all relieved to be fans rather than board members.

'I don't miss it,' says Taylor. 'Being a supporter of a football club is so much more enjoyable than being a director. Like all City fans this season, I marvel at the human shield of Morgan and Huth, Mahrez's skill, Kante's tackling, Vardy's goals and Drinkwater's passing but the real joy is in watching the teamwork involved because the output is greater than the sum of the parts.

'Opposing teams know how we play. It's been analysed to death by the pundits yet, to date, few have been able to suppress the exuberance and confidence of eleven footballers playing to win.'

Taylor began supporting City in 1976 during the days of Weller, Worthington and Birchenall.

Jon Holmes goes back much further.

'My dad used to give the bloke on the turnstiles half a crown,' says Holmes. 'I was lifted over and I used to sit between my father and my grandfather.

'I remember when we played Spurs in 1963 and there were people all along the top of the Burnmoor Street stand.'

Over fifty years on, City are again battling with Tottenham for the league title.

'Whatever happens, it's been a fantastic season. I've been to nine away games. We've won every bloody one of them. It's unbelievable.'

'It's like a dream you never envisaged yourself having,' says Johnson. 'It has given me a huge sense of pride. Pride in the club, pride in the team, pride in the fans and pride in the city of Leicester and its people.'

30: NEWCASTLE UNITED (H)

Monday 14 March 2016

WHEN YOUR TEAM IS ON THE VERGE OF HISTORY, LITTLE THINGS seem to make all the difference. In the week leading up to their visit to the King Power, Newcastle United remove their manager Steve McClaren from his post after just nine months in charge and replace him with the former Real Madrid and Liverpool manager Rafael Benítez . Suddenly, what looked like a routine home win appears a tough assignment.

It's the 'new manager bounce' that scares City fans – the inevitable victory brought about by a change at the top. Even a draw would be a handy result for a Newcastle side scrapping with Norwich and Sunderland to claim seventeenth place and another year in the Premier League.

What would a draw be for City? Disastrous? In the context of this improbable title tilt, the answer is yes. It would be disastrous to drop points at home to a team in the bottom three at this stage of the season. Yet, as shown by recent results – Arsenal's home defeat to Swansea; Manchester City's goalless draw at Norwich two days ago – even the most expensively assembled sides can fail. That's what makes all the predictions so pointless and the two months ahead so agonising.

It is widely assumed that Benítez will sharpen his new side's resolve, organise them and make them harder to beat. In their past two visits to this corner of the East Midlands, they could barely have made it any easier. In January 2015, a second-string City team strolled to a 1-0 defeat in the FA Cup which sparked anger from the black-and-white striped corner of the stadium. The following May, their supposedly strongest selection conceded three goals and lost two men to red cards. Even on their patch earlier this season, it was the same story: 3-0 to City and one of the easiest afternoons of the campaign. Seven goals without reply in three games. No wonder we were confident before the arrival of Benítez.

The Spaniard's presence in the opposition dugout is an unforeseen obstacle, just something else blocking the path to glory.

This isn't a well-trodden path for Leicester City and the players and fans are learning together as it winds towards a conclusion. This evening's lesson reinforces the growing sense that the performance is no longer important. At this stage of the season, it's all about winning.

Earlier in the season, it was vital for Ranieri to work out his best side. That process involved a series of trials for the likes of Ritchie De Laet, Gökhan Inler and Leonardo Ulloa, but also for Danny Simpson, Danny Drinkwater and even N'Golo Kanté. Points were proven by a number of players with excellent individual and team displays, earning them the right to see out the season. Even the odd dip in performance levels has not seen Ranieri shuffle his pack. There is a very clear first eleven.

Those eleven names are all on the teamsheet for the visit of Newcastle: Schmeichel; Simpson, Morgan, Huth, Fuchs; Mahrez, Drinkwater, Kanté, Albrighton; Okazaki, Vardy.

Eleven men effectively charged with winning City's first ever top flight title. In the short term, that means beating Newcastle to restore a five-point advantage over Tottenham. Whatever it takes to win. The performance is irrelevant. Fortunately.

City don't play well, but we still win. The confidence, trust and knowledge built between Ranieri's squad proves enough to propel them to these kind of victories. Again, the back four are rock solid and offer few opportunities to the visitors. Again, it only takes one goal.

With Jamie Vardy struggling to find the same space he was afforded before opponents realised his status as one of the league's foremost goalscoring threats, it's up to others to put the ball in the back of the net. Ulloa did it against Norwich. Mahrez did it against Watford. Twenty minutes in, Shinji Okazaki does it against Newcastle by meeting Vardy's knock-down with an acrobatic overhead kick from close range to score his first goal at the King Power.

Despite Benítez organising his new side effectively, they struggle to break City down. There are few events of note in a poor game, particularly a second half that will be quickly forgotten after the final whistle. Thankfully, that's just what is needed in this scenario. We don't need wonderful memories. We just need three points. And then three more. And then three more.

Three minutes of injury time are spent in the corner of the pitch closest to the Union FS section. Every time substitute Jeff Schlupp plays the ball against a Newcastle defender to win another throw-in or corner, a roar goes up from the whole stadium. The roar that greets the final whistle is even louder but a hush soon descends as the supporters file out, in contrast to the raucous celebrations after the 1-0 win at Vicarage Road nine days earlier. Reality is starting to dawn and it's enough to leave anyone speechless.

Leicester City 1 (Okazaki)

Newcastle United 0

Team: Schmeichel, Simpson, Morgan, Huth, Fuchs, Mahrez, Drinkwater, Kanté, Albrighton (Ulloa), Okazaki (Schlupp), Vardy

THE OUTSIDE BET

'FIRSTLY,' SAYS CHRIS, A LIFELONG CITY FROM GROBY, 'I'M NOT really a betting person. So when I do bet, I've always tried to look for a decent return.

'In 1985, I put a pound on Liverpool to do the double. They were mid-table at the time, so the odds were 100/1. It came through. I had to ask my dad to go to the betting shop to pick it up as I was too young. He said it was the easiest money he ever made.'

100/1 is one thing. Leicester City were 5,000/1 to win the Premier League at the start of the 2015/16 season and the odds didn't exactly tumble despite the team's excellent early form.

Chris placed the bet of his life.

'The biggest chunk of my winnings came from a 2,000/1 each-way bet that I placed after six games,' he says. 'It just goes to show how much people thought this whole Leicester thing was only a blip and we would soon fall away.

'On top of that I had put a fiver on us in pre-season to win the title outright at 2,500/1 and a fiver on a 250/1 top four finish. The time I put the pre-season bets on, I was actually going to put fifty quid on the outright win. I made the cautious error of asking opinions of those in the office whose general sentiment was 'well, if you're going to throw your money away', so I only went with a tenth of the stake.'

Many fans who placed bets on City to win the league had carefully considered the possibility rather than seeing it as a shot to nothing.

'There were a few things that caused me to be optimistic,' says Chris. 'Firstly, we adapted quickly to situations that needed fixing. Our leaky defence early on became one of the meanest in the league. Also, Ranieri has proved to be very professional and quick to realise when his own preferences have not been best for the team.

Chris began to believe his optimism was well-founded before the trip to the Etihad Stadium in February for a game he was convinced we would win.

'I put a tenner on us to win 3-0 at 120/1,' he says. 'I remember sitting there watching the cash-out button sitting at £650 as Agüero scored in the 87th minute to make it 3-1. Perhaps this is why I have become more open to the idea of taking the return while you can!'

Ah yes, the cash-out option. It is impossible to watch any live football on television these days without someone – usually Ray Winstone – imploring you to cash out.

Chris did just that with the majority of his bets and pocketed just over £17,000.

There were a few reasons behind his decision to take the money, the main one being Tottenham's game at whipping boys Aston Villa being scheduled before City's home game against Newcastle United. The nerves would have been too much.

'There were other minor factors,' says Chris. 'Benítez came in at Newcastle and I heard on the radio that only four out of the current twenty Premier League managers lost their first game.

'There was also pressure from my family to take the money and not risk it going any further. I'm still, of course, wondering whether I made the right decision. Whatever happens, I will have come away with something. I do still want Leicester to win the Premier League!'

Chris has set aside part of his winnings to continue supporting City.

'I'd love to do a couple of Champions League away legs,' he says. 'The last time I went to something like that was when I lived in Milan in the mid-nineties and Aston Villa came over to play Inter Milan in the UEFA Cup. We sat in the home end of the San Siro amongst a furnace of fireworks, trying desperately not to speak English while surrounded by Italians screaming all kinds of obscenities at the English players.

'I'm also buying a dog for my son. He has always wanted a dog and at the start of the season I told him I would buy him one if Leicester won the league. This has also had the added benefit of getting him interested in Leicester City, which has been tough before with him living down in London.'

City are heading to the capital themselves and thousands of us will be along for the ride. We're off to a very familiar venue.

31: CRYSTAL PALACE (A)

Saturday 19 March 2016

THE HEART SAYS VICTORY AND THE HEAD SAYS DEFEAT AT Selhurst Park. Or should that be the other way round?

There are so many reasons to believe and so many reasons to fear.

Crystal Palace haven't won any of their previous twelve league games, only managing to draw four of them. As a result, they have been sliding down the table at an alarming rate after sitting sixth at Christmas just nine points behind league leaders Leicester City. The team at the top remains the same but Palace have since slumped to fifteenth and the gap between the two is now 30 points.

All of that should be reason for optimism, but some of us are eternal pessimists. Blame Francis Benali, the Southampton defender who played 389 times and scored once. That goal came against Leicester City. A Benali goal was so infrequent, or otherwise non-existent to be more precise, that one football statistics website rounds his goals-per-games ratio down and lists it as 0.00. But thousands of us were there at The Dell when he looped a header into the corner of Kasey Keller's net to give Saints a 2-0 lead. There's a Vine of the goal which you can watch on a loop. No doubt Benali has watched it more than once. More than 389 times.

So many supporters of football clubs outside the elite think like this, that their club is doomed to fail at the worst possible time and can list a number of strikers who broke a goal drought against their side.

There's more substance to this creeping sense of unease about Selhurst Park though, for this is the venue where the last unlikely title contenders – Brendan Rodgers' Liverpool side of 2014 – saw their bid for glory suffer a damaging blow. A team including Luis Suárez, Steven Gerrard, Raheem Sterling and Daniel Sturridge led 3-0 but Palace fought back to secure a draw and place the trophy firmly within Manchester City's grasp.

Leicester City aren't just unlikely title contenders though. Leicester City are unbelievable title contenders. We've been to Selhurst many times but never like this.

Two defeats at Crystal Palace are particularly memorable.

On 7 August 2010, opening-day optimism under new manager Paulo Sousa was deflated by a 3-0 half-time deficit. City were better in the second half and scored twice without reply to force a nervy conclusion but the damage had been done.

On 27 September 2014, City arrived in south London on the back of an unforgettable 5-3 win over Manchester United. Palace won 2-0. We didn't win again until after Christmas, a run that necessitated the greatest of escapes.

It's no wonder there are nerves about playing the only team in the league that haven't won yet in 2016.

At least interest lies in the Premier League's lunch-time kick-off – third-placed Arsenal's trip to Goodison Park – rather than the Championship's offering of Derby County against Nottingham Forest, a fixture that has never seemed less appealing.

The buses and coaches pull up on Park Road and City fans spill out onto the pavement, joined by hundreds more to have travelled by car or train. We pass through turnstiles into the open-air concourse. Palace, like most clubs, put on an unnecessary welcome to 'enhance the matchday experience'. The City badge is displayed above our heads. The staff serving gourmet burgers and salads wear shirts with Gary Lineker's face on them. It's an odd touch. More importantly, Arsenal are winning 2-0 at Everton, a lead they maintain comfortably until the final whistle.

In the middle of the last decade, Selhurst Park felt like the setting for an annual and inevitable defeat. The location of the visitors' section has changed during that time from the left side of the Arthur Wait Stand that runs along one side of the pitch to the stand behind the goal opposite the Holmesdale Road End and finally back to the right side of the Arthur Wait Stand. The price has gone up too, although the view has never got any better. Forty pounds is the price for this trip to south London, even for those placed directly behind a pillar that obscures the entire centre circle.

It turns out the levels of customer service don't extend from the concourse into the stand.

'It's sold out, mate. What do you want me to do? Remove the pillar?'

The game kicks off, presumably.

It's a choice between peering either side of the pillar or looking up at the big screen behind Kasper Schmeichel's goal every time the ball goes into midfield. It won't matter as long as City win.

The views might be the worst in the Premier League but the acoustics are among the best. It's noisy. City start well with the same relentless energy that we've come to expect. Riyad Mahrez wastes a glorious chance after being put clean through by a defence-splitting ball from England's newest call-up, Danny Drinkwater.

All the doubters are right, in a way. City's players don't look like they're part of a title-chasing team. They look like one fighting relegation. That is to say, they look desperate. They look like they did at this point last season when the great escape was in motion.

So many players embody that approach but Marc Albrighton is worth singling out. Palace's threat comes from their tricky wingers, Wilfried Zaha and Yannick Bolasie, and Albrighton is quick to help his full-back, Christian Fuchs, in dealing with Zaha. Bolasie is playing more centrally but when he drifts wide, Riyad Mahrez gets back to support Danny Simpson. In the middle, Robert Huth and Wes Morgan achieve the improbable and make a six-foot-four man, Emmanuel Adebayor, look invisible.

City just need a goal, which arrives ten minutes before half time. Drinkwater picks out Albrighton with a clever lofted pass and Albrighton takes the ball across the edge of the area from the left before giving it to Mahrez on the right. Mahrez's cross is easily cleared but it falls to Drinkwater once more. This time there's a bit of space for Jamie Vardy, who occupies the left channel vacated by Albrighton and his marker Joel Ward. Drinkwater plays in Vardy and the striker works an angle to drive the ball across the box.

Mahrez, sprinting into the danger zone after his earlier cross, finishes side-footed past the diving Wayne Hennessey to put City one up. The celebration among the away fans, like the one that greeted Mahrez's winner at Watford, is longer and louder than normal. A goal isn't just an opener these days for Leicester City. It's so often the winner as well.

The interplay between City's front four is a joy to watch. Both wingers drift inside, Shinji Okazaki drops deep and Vardy stretches the back line. Drinkwater pulls the strings. N'Golo Kanté mops up any loose balls. It's a recipe for success – so simple and yet so effective.

However, this match is really all about the five men further back. Simpson and Fuchs do an excellent job of curtailing the dribbles of the lively Zaha and Bolasie, forcing them to whip cross after cross straight to City's commanding central defenders, Morgan and Huth. During a series of late corners for the home side, roared into the box by the Holmesdale Road end behind the goal, the ball seems to be magnetically attracted to Morgan. When Palace do get through, Kasper Schmeichel's handling is flawless. This ground, a graveyard for so many title hopes, holds no fear for the likes of Schmeichel and Morgan, who played here regularly in the Championship.

There are still fine margins. There always are when a team is protecting a one-goal lead away from home. Substitute Leonardo Ulloa comes close to turning the ball past his own goalkeeper before the Palace centre-back Damien Delaney hooks an injury time volley onto the top of the bar. Schmeichel spreads his arms out wide as soon as Delaney makes contact, supremely confident that his clean sheet will remain intact. From the visiting supporters' section one hundred yards away, it didn't look quite so obvious. A huge sigh of relief goes up as the ball bounces off the bar and behind.

Each time the final whistle goes with City leading, it feels like the most important sound in the world. This one is beautiful. Even before it happens, the sight of the referee lifting his whistle when there is no possible reason other than to end the game is truly special.

The most memorable part of the afternoon is still to come. Mahrez's goal felt good. The final whistle felt great. What follows is unforgettable.

Someone starts a chant.

'We're gonna win the league... we're gonna win the league...'

It's been sung before. Others join in.

'I know you won't believe us,' sing some supporters.

'And now you're gonna believe us,' sing others.

Whether others believe or not, this is the strongest signal possible that the fans now truly believe.

'We're gonna win the league,' we all sing together.

And it goes on. And on. And on. For around fifteen minutes. Nobody is leaving the away end. Grinning children are held aloft. Flags are raised. Scarves are twirled. The noise grows.

'We're gonna win the league... we're gonna win the league...'

Eventually, above the din, there is an electronic xylophone sound, as though someone is about to announce that the train arriving into platform five is the 17:32 to Bristol Temple Meads.

A voice comes over the Tannoy system. It pleads with the City fans to leave the stadium. We're having none of it.

'We shall not… we shall not be moved…'

Eventually, we do move. But those twenty minutes or so spent inside Selhurst Park at the end of another gripping game will live long in the memory of everyone who experienced them.

And there's nothing Francis Benali can do about it.

Crystal Palace 0

Leicester City 1 (Mahrez)

Team: Schmeichel, Simpson, Morgan, Huth, Fuchs, Mahrez (Schlupp), Drinkwater, Kanté, Albrighton, Okazaki (Ulloa), Vardy (Amartey)

THE TWO LIONS

IT'S NOT EVEN MIDDAY. SOME PEOPLE ARE ALREADY ON THEIR second pint and they're not drinking water. St Patrick's Day. Amid the mass of green, surely one or two Leicester City fans are raising their glasses to toast the man they love more than he'll ever know. At 11.30am on Thursday 17 March 2016, Danny Drinkwater receives his first-ever call-up to the England squad – his name listed alongside that of his team-mate Jamie Vardy.

Less than a year ago, it seemed unlikely. Less than three years ago, it seemed unthinkable.

On the opening day of the 2013/14 season, Nigel Pearson took his City side to Middlesbrough for a tough Championship encounter.

This was the team – spot the current heroes: Schmeichel, St Ledger, Morgan, Whitbread (Moore), De Laet, James, Drinkwater, King, Konchesky, Wood (Nugent), Vardy.

Two moved to the Championship, another two are on loan at Championship clubs, one plays in League One and another in Major League Soccer in the United States.

Seven remain at the club, four of whom have been virtually ever-present in City's title charge.

Now two of them are in the England squad.

Looking back, that sunny afternoon in the north east was the turning point. City had fallen apart in the closing months of the previous season, tumbling from the top of the Championship to scrape a play-off place. Danny Drinkwater and Jamie Vardy began the fateful final game at Vicarage Road on the bench alongside their current international colleague Harry Kane.

The first game of the following campaign was vital, and many fans were furious at the inclusion of Drinkwater and Vardy. The first half appeared to prove them right, with both players struggling as Middlesbrough took a lead they maintained until the break. Then Drinkwater equalised, Vardy scored the winner and City won the game. We won 30 more on the way to a club record 102 points and promotion to the Premier League. Supporters voted Drinkwater as Player of the Year, while the City squad voted Vardy as theirs. The unlikely lads were back on track.

This week, England will play two friendlies: world champions Germany in Berlin on Saturday; the Netherlands, who have not qualified for the European Championships, at Wembley on Tuesday.

We begin in Berlin. Thousands of Leicester City fans watch the match on television. There are some inside the stadium. There is one who is even closer to the action.

Getty Images' Michael Regan is the England team photographer.

'Germany v England was the 128th England match I'd covered,' says Michael. 'Seeing a Leicester player in the squad felt surreal at first. Now there were two. I'd shot the match against Belgium at Sunderland in 1999 when Emile Heskey and Steve Guppy had played but it was so long ago I'd long forgotten what it felt like to see Leicester City represented so well with England.'

With twenty minutes remaining, Germany lead 2-1. Roy Hodgson brings Vardy on for his fifth appearance in an England shirt.

'When Vardy came on as a substitute the first thing I noticed was the reception the England fans gave him. 'Jamie Vardy's having a party' struck up before he even got on the grass. There was a lot of negativity about his initial call up but the England fans who actually turn up at games had taken to him straight away. Before I knew it he'd backheeled a half-volley past the best keeper in the world.'

Nathaniel Clyne raids down the right and fires in a low cross. Vardy gets in front of his marker Antonio Rüdiger to meet the ball first. He flicks it with his right foot behind his standing foot and it zips past Manuel Neuer into the net.

On the side of the pitch, Michael processes what he has just seen.

'My first emotion was to worry if I had the picture,' he says. 'The second emotion was pride as a Leicester fan and a distant third was delight that we'd come back from two goals down against the world champions in their backyard.

'It must have felt pretty surreal to the England fans watching at home or in the stadium, incomprehensible even that a Leicester player had turned up and pulled that off in such style. As a Leicester fan, maybe for the first time, I felt like I was starting to get used to it.'

Vardy puffs out his cheeks and spreads his arms wide in celebration. Drinkwater, warming up on the other side of the pitch from Michael, punches the air. Leicester City flags hang proudly from the upper tier at the far end. England go on to score a last-minute winner and City's number nine has helped to change the game.

'It's definitely the high point of the season,' says Vardy in his post-match interview. A record-breaking goal against Manchester United and a wonder strike against Liverpool must vie for second place, and there's yet more competition to come three days later.

Vardy and Drinkwater are both named in the starting line up against the Netherlands. There is an emotional tribute to the incomparable Johan Cruyff, who passed away in the week leading up to the game. He would have appreciated the beauty and invention of Vardy's goal in Berlin.

Drinkwater settles quickly into the very different role he has been given in the England team, pulling the strings in front of the back four with short, sharp passes and diligent defensive work. There are no lofted through balls over the Dutch defence for Vardy to chase and there is no N'Golo Kanté to cover any runs forward. Kanté is busy enjoying his full debut for France in Paris and scoring the opening goal against Russia on his 25th birthday. News of that goal is received almost as warmly among City fans as the one which gives England the lead towards the end of an uneventful first half.

It's a far more simple finish for Vardy this time. A slick England move sets Kyle Walker free on the right and his cross finds Vardy in plenty of space inside the penalty area. The ball hits the roof of the Dutch net and City's star striker has two goals in two games.

The Netherlands score twice in the second half to win the game but that does little to dampen our mood as Drinkwater is named Man of the Match and Vardy takes another step closer to securing a place in the squad for the European Championships. Claudio Ranieri watches on proudly from the stands and City fans across the globe think back to that day in Middlesbrough less than three years earlier when two future England stars began to prove everybody wrong.

32: SOUTHAMPTON (H)

Sunday 3 April 2016

WE LOOK FOR SIGNS, FOR OMENS, FOR ANYTHING TO CALM the nerves. How's this? Leicester City's four fixtures in April – Southampton, West Ham United and Swansea City at home; Sunderland away – also all took place during the great escape last season. Both then and in the reverse fixtures earlier this season, City took ten points out of twelve. A repeat this month would take Ranieri's men to 76 points with three games to play and surely place the title within reach.

It's an obsession and yet so unthinkable that it's hard to comprehend. These should be enjoyable times. They're certainly stressful for many of us.

Saturday's late kick-off sees second-placed Tottenham Hotspur make the trip to Anfield and we're all Liverpool fans for 90 minutes. Philippe Coutinho gives the home side the lead but a precise Harry Kane strike draws Spurs level and the gap is cut to four points.

The international break offered timely respite from the nerves but we must now wait to see its effect on our players. Perhaps the emphasis is on those who did not travel to play for their countries – the likes of Danny Simpson, Robert Huth, Marc Albrighton and Leonardo Ulloa – to step up and lighten the load on their colleagues.

On the Raw Dykes Road that leads to the stadium, a man wearing a Chelsea shirt tries to drum up interest in scarves proclaiming Leicester City to be 2015/16 Premiership champions. Quite apart from the fact it hasn't been called the Premiership for years, there's so much wrong with that scene that all we can do is shake our heads and walk on.

Thankfully, free beer and doughnuts are on offer for City fans to celebrate our chairman's birthday. Gestures like this could make a difference. Southampton's visit to the King Power is the first of three successive games to kick off at half past one on a Sunday afternoon. Anything that might help to boost the atmosphere is welcome, given that the vast majority of fans will not be as well-oiled as usual.

As we bite into our doughnuts, the hot topic is the morning's Sunday Times report that players connected with City are among those linked to a widespread doping scandal. No individuals are named and there seems very little evidence to support the claims, which makes the timing of the article all the more frustrating. City are one of three Premier League clubs, along with Arsenal and Chelsea, forced to release a statement denying the accusations.

The chairman's birthday is a big deal. A huge flag is unveiled in the East Stand with a celebratory message. If that seems like a grand gesture, it pales into insignificance compared to the aeroplane that starts to circle the stadium pulling a banner reading: 'Happy birthday'. All of this will seem hollow if City fail to win.

After half an hour of competitive football with few opportunities at either end, there are two flashpoints that decide the game.

With 31 minutes on the clock, Graziano Pellè plays a perfectly-timed through ball to set Sadio Mané through on goal from the halfway line. Mané, a highly-rated Senegalese international who has been linked heavily with Manchester United, has the pace to get away from Danny Simpson and soon finds himself with just Kasper Schmeichel to beat. He knocks the ball to his right and finds the angle to shoot.

An open goal surely awaits, but Mané elects to shoot as soon as Schmeichel is taken out of the equation. Simpson has made a magnificent recovery. Mané lifts the ball straight into his path and, although the ball hits his elbow and Southampton manager Ronald Koeman will later claim it to be a clear penalty, there is nothing Simpson can do about it. Nothing he can do but sigh with relief and listen to the standing ovation he receives from tens of thousands of City fans. This is what we love. We will always acclaim anyone who gives one hundred per cent to the shirt. When there is so much at stake, it means even more.

Seven minutes later, Mané is probably still thinking about his inability to find a way past Simpson when two other City defenders combine to make his afternoon even worse. The opportunity is worked from the left, reminiscent of the build up to the Christian Fuchs cross at Watford that led to Riyad Mahrez's winner. Fuchs again finds himself in a surprising amount of space and whips in a bedevilling cross. Wes Morgan isn't favourite to win it in the air but he eases the Dutch midfielder Jordy Clasie out of his way before powering a header towards the near post.

It takes something special to beat Southampton's number one, the England international Fraser Forster, and this is it. The giant Forster dives but cannot stop the ball reaching the net. The captain has timed his first goal of the season perfectly. For the third game in a row, City go in at half time with a one-goal lead to protect.

The likes of Simpson and Morgan have been damned with faint praise by the media for much of the season, continually marked down as players who give their all and love defending. Surely these qualities should be the bare minimum we ask of our footballers? It's reductive to suggest that City's back line consists of lower league cloggers who have struck lucky.

What we see after the break, as Southampton push for an equaliser, is worthy of higher praise. City are on the back foot for almost the entirety of a tense second half but Ranieri's well-drilled defensive line stands firm. Saints have plenty of possession on the edge of the City penalty area. Schmeichel has very little to do.

It seems City can't score two goals in one game these days so even when Jamie Vardy motors away from the Southampton defence on the left and pokes the ball across to Simpson at the back post, it's no surprise when Forster makes a stupendous save. Simpson holds his head in his hands. What a time it would have been to register his first goal for the club.

We haven't enjoyed the luxury of a two-goal lead for nearly two months. We're used to this now. It's still tense. Substitutes Demarai Gray and Leonardo Ulloa play their part by holding the ball in the corner to help see out five minutes of stoppage time. At the final whistle, cardboard clappers rain down from the stands and there are clenched fists on and off the pitch.

We played our part in this one. The noise was deafening at times. Our players don't need drugs and neither do we. There's no feeling like this. It's agonising and gut-wrenching and it makes us feel ill but what a time to be alive.

Southampton are an excellent team. Their strength in depth is unquestionable. Seventeen of their players were on international duty prior to their visit to the King Power. So what is setting City apart from teams like Southampton at the moment? There are key moments in games like Simpson's block and Morgan's goal where fine margins are going in City's favour, but this isn't luck. It's a team packed with talented footballers who are playing like they're fans. Ranieri has told his side to play every game as though it's their last. He wants them to be desperate and when they're not desperate, they're not Leicester. It's music to our ears.

As the sun goes down with City seven points clear at the top of the Premier League, it's impossible not to look back at the league table exactly one year ago. Seven points adrift. All looked lost. Since then, we have played 41 Premier League games and taken 91 points, eighteen more than any other club during the same period.

We still search for anything that can calm the nerves. For many, not even a win will do it. We're already thinking about the next game.

Leicester City 1 (Morgan)

Southampton 0

Team: Schmeichel, Simpson, Morgan, Huth, Fuchs, Mahrez (Gray), Drinkwater, Kanté, Albrighton (Dyer), Okazaki (Ulloa), Vardy

THE LEGEND

EMILE HESKEY WAS JUST SEVENTEEN YEARS OLD WHEN HE MADE his Leicester City debut on 8 March 1995. It would be the only game he played that season – a 2-0 defeat to Queens Park Rangers at Loftus Road – as City were relegated after a solitary year in the Premier League.

'I wasn't told I was playing until just before the kick-off so I didn't have time to get excited,' says Heskey. 'We had a lot of players who were sick that day and I'd travelled a couple of times with the team so I got my opportunity. It wasn't the best of debuts but it put me in good stead to go forward.

'Getting that one game was a nice introduction.'

Heskey was still a teenager when he was back in the top flight following promotion under Martin O'Neill in 1996. Although a very different type of player to Jamie Vardy, with strength and height in his armoury as well as startling pace, Heskey was similar in the way he led from the front and showed no fear when visiting the most intimidating venues in England.

City finished in the top half of the Premier League four years in a row, but it was League Cup success in 1997 and 2000 that Heskey recalls with the greatest affection.

'The best feeling was winning the cups,' he says. 'Especially the first one. I scored the goal at Wembley that took it to a replay. We played at Hillsborough and Stevie Claridge scored the winner. They were great days.'

Lots of City fans compare the team Martin O'Neill built, of which Heskey was an integral part, to the side of today – a combination of players discarded from bigger clubs or making their way up from the lower leagues. They had one quality which bound them together.

'We had belief,' says Heskey. 'Belief in ourselves. Belief in the team. We had a camaraderie and we knew what we were capable of doing. We had that every year.

'It's only when you look back at it that you think we achieved a lot. Possibly we overachieved but when you're in and amongst it, it's what you expect that you, as players, are capable of.

'This season, Leicester have played with a similar sort of belief. They play with the same team spirit that we did. Even more so. They're confident they can win every game. Everyone's pulling together.

'The passing and possession stats aren't the best but they play counter-attacking football that works well for the players they have. Everyone knows their job and everyone does their job well.'

Heskey appears to retain inherent belief in the current City side and can't pick one moment when they suddenly looked like title contenders.

'I haven't seen anything out of the ordinary,' he says. 'I've seen players and a team playing together with a respect and an understanding for each other, aware of what they want to achieve and once you have that, you get results.

'I thought Christmas time would bring the defining moment. You've got so many games and they come thick and fast. Once you get into it, you can start drawing or losing games you should be winning. It gets difficult after that but Leicester went from strength to strength. They had the odd setback but bounced straight back from them every time. Three losses so far throughout the whole season is an amazing feat.'

It has been amazing and Leicester City are now closer to glory than ever before. This is a whole new level, but the O'Neill team showed a glimpse of similar potential. One sunny day in March 2000, Heskey and Stan Collymore destroyed Sunderland. Collymore scored a hat-trick and Heskey got a goal too. It looked like the perfect partnership. Then, just when City looked capable of building on a solid foundation and pushing on towards European qualification through the Premier League, Heskey left.

'You always have the feeling that you might move on at some stage, especially if you carry on doing well,' he says. 'That Sunderland game was special for me though because I got to play alongside Stan.

'When I was younger I was told to watch Stan constantly. He was wonderful for Forest and Liverpool and to play alongside him was great. It was a big disappointment that we never got to play together for longer, but it was nice for that one game.'

The prospect of facing Sunderland brings special memories for Leicester City fans. Now, as we prepare for the long journey north to face the Mackems, it's just another game. Another game to negotiate on the way to our players achieving something no Leicester City legend has ever managed before.

33: SUNDERLAND (A)

Sunday 10 April 2016

THREE THOUSAND OF US TRAVEL TO SUNDERLAND FOR ONE OF the most important games we will ever see. They're all like that now. Some set off on Friday to make a weekend of it, while others head up on Saturday to go out for a few drinks. The rest of us set our alarm clocks for stupid o'clock and fish out sat-navs or dog-eared road atlases.

As we make our way up the M1, we pass by names from our past.

Junction 24: Derby and Nottingham.

This is the life City left behind. The nerves of an East Midlands rivalry. The workplace one-upmanship. The clubs at either end of Brian Clough Way battling it out in the Championship.

There's been little enjoyment recently for Nottingham Forest fans. Their team won three times in the first three months of the season, before threatening to start rising up the table with a 1-0 win over Derby. They lost at Brentford but then went unbeaten for twelve league matches.

Briefly, things looked rosy for the Reds. Their manager, Dougie Freedman, appeared to be getting the best out of his players and they rose to tenth in the Championship table, within reach of the play-offs. A 2-0 defeat at home to Huddersfield Town sparked another slump though, this time consisting of eight defeats in ten games. Freedman departed in the middle of that awful run and, as City prepare to face Sunderland seemingly on the verge of creating history, life as a Nottingham Forest fan must feel bleak.

They don't care about Leicester City, as they keep reminding us on a regular basis. They only care about Derby County, who haven't had the season they were hoping for either.

Derby's prospects look slightly brighter. Ahead of the weekend, their expensively-assembled squad is clinging onto the sixth and final play-off place with six games remaining. There were high hopes for Paul Clement, who had previously been assistant manager at Real Madrid, but he was soon shown the door as the club's hierarchy despaired at his inability to implement the so-called 'Derby way'.

Some of us, crazy that we are, thought we would miss one or two aspects of life in the Football League. As our team prepares to try extending its Premier League lead to ten points, the thought of a Championship fixture against Derby or Forest is not top of our agenda.

Junction 33: Sheffield

The journey continues. The coaches roll on through old coalmine territories, past the lower-league towns of Chesterfield and Mansfield and the familiar recent venues of Doncaster and Barnsley, until the view out of the windows on the left side becomes a vast, sprawling industrial city surrounded by hills on all sides. Sheffield: another regular destination during City's decade away from the top flight. From removing our shoes at Bramall Lane to hailing Gary Megson at Hillsborough, the steel city has provided some memorable away days in the past ten years but it has mostly brought defeat.

Sheffield Wednesday are battling it out along with Derby to secure a play-off place. Sheffield United, meanwhile, look set to miss out on the League One play-offs and remain out of the top two divisions for a sixth consecutive season – a reminder of what can happen if promotion is not achieved from the third tier at the first attempt.

Thank heavens for that Wednesday legend, Nigel Pearson.

Junction 43: Leeds.

If Nottingham Forest have become accustomed to failure and Sheffield United are becalmed in League One, then what is there to say about Leeds United?

Leeds, historically a gigantic club with tales to tell of their feared sides of the past, have been stumbling from one crisis to another for years. Just over a year ago, it was

Leicester City that appeared to be in crisis. What a difference twelve months can make. The owners, management team, players and supporters of Leicester City are, unlike Leeds, united.

The cars and coaches go on until, at long last, we reach the Stadium of Light and memories of our previous visit come flooding back.

'That will do for Leicester. There have been some special ones, but this has to go down as the greatest relegation escape the Premier League has ever known': the words of Match of the Day commentator Guy Mowbray at the final whistle in City's goalless draw at Sunderland in May 2015 that confirmed our Premier League status for another year.

What a sweet sound that whistle made. Esteban Cambiasso picked up the ball and held it out in front of him. The City players congregated in celebration. Even Jeff Schlupp eventually realised what the result meant. High up above Kasper Schmeichel's goal, we went wild with delight.

It's not the benefit of hindsight that allows the greatest of escapes to be viewed as an opportunity for this team to kick on and make the most of their talent. It was always true. That's what was frustrating about the majority of last season. We knew they were capable of so much more. We just didn't realise quite how far they would take us on what has been a magical journey to this point.

A draw was the minimum we needed that day. Only a win will do today.

It's bobble hat and sunglasses weather – chilly but bright. Hundreds of fans stand outside the Colliery Tavern with pints in hand, enjoying the sun and showing no signs of tension. Sunderland are one of several clubs to follow a similar format with their so-called fan zone, a gated section outside the stadium where supporters of both clubs mingle while a local band turns the amp up to eleven only to receive general disinterest in return.

Ranieri picks his usual eleven.

Sunderland's main threat – perhaps only threat, though we cannot bring ourselves to jinx anything – is Jermain Defoe, one of the deadliest finishers in Premier League history. It's important we don't give him a sniff. We trust in Wes and Huth.

The first half is scrappy but there's some strong intent from City. Shinji Okazaki is lively, although his touch lets him down at vital times – perhaps an able summary of his efforts in a blue shirt all season. The star attackers, Jamie Vardy and Riyad Mahrez, are less involved and it soon becomes clear this will be a tough afternoon. Sunderland don't offer a lot up front but their defence holds firm and there are few opportunities for either side.

Perhaps the main talking point is referee Anthony Taylor's failure to award Okazaki a penalty after the Japanese striker takes the ball on his chest in the area only to be prevented from shooting by the home side's right-back DeAndre Yedlin. Taylor presumably sees it as a 'coming together'. From high up in the away end, it's difficult to tell. Those watching on television are treated to numerous replays showing Yedlin kicking Okazaki in the chest.

The game remains in the balance into the second half. From the back of the visiting supporters' section, we can't see a clock inside the stadium because of the overhanging roof. It feels like time has stopped still. Occasionally we remember to check our watches or our phones but there's so much happening on the pitch that nobody wants to tear their eyes away from the action.

To the neutral, there may not seem to be much action. You never know what might be decisive though. A routine pass or tackle in the middle of the park could prove the moment when the pendulum swings in favour of one team or the other.

Perhaps we'll play forever until someone scores.

Halfway through the second half, someone does score.

Riyad Mahrez, who has scored the winner in City's last two away games, is clearly having an off-day, one of those afternoons when defenders are closing down his usual languid lope and he begins to look lazy. There's no joy from set pieces either – Sunderland are a giant side able to cope with the aerial threat of Morgan and Huth. Ranieri's men have consistently found different ways to win games, so it's time to go back to what worked so well on several occasions last autumn.

Danny Drinkwater picks up possession in midfield and plays the long ball early, stabbing at it with his right foot to ensure it holds up when it lands rather than running through to the goalkeeper. He's tried this more than once already today with no success but this time Jamie Vardy has managed to isolate his marker, Younes Kaboul, on the halfway line. The ball drops in the left channel and Vardy is onto it in a flash, while Kaboul hesitates before giving chase. You can't give Jamie Vardy a headstart in a race. It's difficult enough when he starts ten yards behind you.

Vardy takes a touch and it looks too heavy, just as it did back in the summer of 2013 when his winner at Middlesbrough began to turn his career around. Sunderland goalkeeper Vito Mannone has made the same mistake as Kaboul though. He's hesitated. Vardy gets to the ball first and lifts it past Mannone into the net.

Leicester City have been accused of playing long ball football this season. Pundits have said it isn't easy on the eye, while eulogising over Tottenham Hotspur's pretty patterns in possession.

Tell that to the thousands of City fans who go up and down the country every other week and watch Jamie Vardy racing onto a through ball, beating the defender with sheer pace and slotting into the bottom corner.

It's beautiful.

Nothing can beat it. The thrill of the chase you know the defender will never win; the look of anxiety on the goalkeeper's face; the sense of anticipation as Vardy prepares to shoot: you can't replicate that with any number of short passes in the build-up to a goal. It's pure adrenaline and it's addictive. Give us more. Do it again. Let's see it.

For now, City relax.

They still create the odd chance but they also slow the game down. Take the sting out of it. This is Ranieri's influence, of course – closing out the ninety minutes rather than going for the jugular. Demarai Gray and Daniel Amartey both come on to join Leonardo Ulloa, who had replaced Okazaki prior to Vardy's goal, and the three replacements all help to keep the ball in the Sunderland half.

It's become an art form in recent weeks. Gray, in particular, has developed a real knack for it, retaining possession at all costs.

There is one scare. An unfortunate deflection leaves Sunderland substitute Jack Rodwell in front of goal with just Kasper Schmeichel to beat and nearly the entire net at which to aim. Up in the rafters, we wait for it to ripple. The ball travels beyond Schmeichel's reach, up and up. Up. Keep going. It's going to hit the bar. It's still going. Up. Up. Up. And it clears the bar and thousands of City fans collapse with relief and millions of neutrals watching worldwide must do the same.

Panic over, City return to the routine. The ball stays in the Sunderland half and there are no real opportunities for the home side at the other end of the pitch, as though Rodwell's miss has deflated any remaining belief entirely.

City are in the process of seeing out five minutes of injury time fairly comfortably when Vardy decides to end the game himself rather than waiting for the referee's whistle, sprinting clear from halfway to nick the ball past Mannone and roll it into an empty net.

So we can celebrate another brilliant Vardy goal and confirmation of three more crucial points all in one go, and we make a decent fist of it. There are bodies on the floor, bodies in the aisles and limbs all over the place.

Before long, the final whistle has sounded and we're singing again like we did at Selhurst Park. It's not quite the same this time. That was spontaneous and emotional. This feels like the continuing of a tradition. We stay and we sing about winning the league and the magnanimous among the home team's support stay as well to clap us and our players. That takes real class when your own side has just lost an important game that could help to condemn them to relegation.

N'Golo Kanté is named Man of the Match for another incredible display of energy, enthusiasm and destructive midfield play. The question for the opposition is how to prevent him from being so effective. What can managers say to their players?

'That guy who runs around at full pelt all game, tackling anyone in sight and charging up the pitch with the ball… try to avoid him.'

The focus has switched in the past six weeks from an inability to break down Norwich for long periods, through Riyad Mahrez's away-day match winners, favourable refereeing decisions and the brilliance of Wes Morgan, to the fact City haven't conceded a goal for over eight hours.

Those topics have all merited discussion, but the most amazing thing of all has been overlooked. At the precise time when the pressure was meant to tell and teams were supposed to be working out how to stop Leicester City, Claudio Ranieri and his players have won five Premier League games in a row. That's difficult to do at any stage of the season. To do it in mid-April to ensure a seven-point gap at the top with five games left is truly unbelievable.

This whole season is unbelievable.

We get back into our cars and coaches and trains and we make the long journey home, feeling as though we have put in ninety minutes of effort ourselves. We listen to Tottenham's 3-0 win over Manchester United on the way, even more relieved that our team won.

Only when we have returned home do we see that Ranieri was as emotional as many of us at the final whistle.

Speaking in English to the assembled press afterwards, he says: 'It is fantastic when you see before the match, an old lady with a Leicester shirt outside the stadium. I say: 'Unbelievable. They come from Leicester to support us.' This is my emotion. It is fantastic. I was on the bus. I saw them, unbelievable, and I want to say thank you for the support. They are dreaming and we want to continue to dream.'

In an interview with the Italian newspaper Gazzetta dello Sport in his native tongue, Ranieri explains further: 'They weren't real tears, they were unshed tears. It was an emotional moment. Seeing all those people around us, entire families on buses in Leicester shirts to follow us up to Sunderland – that struck me deeply. At times like that you realised the extraordinary power of football. When our sport brings this positivity you can't remain indifferent.'

Sunderland 0

Leicester City 2 (Vardy 2)

Team: Schmeichel, Simpson, Morgan, Huth, Fuchs, Mahrez (Gray), Drinkwater, Kanté, Albrighton (Amartey), Okazaki (Ulloa), Vardy

THE REPORTER

YOUR TEAM IS 3-2 DOWN AT HOME TO MANCHESTER UNITED.
Esteban Cambiasso, newly arrived from Inter Milan and already a hero, slams the
ball into the back of the net to equalise. It's an incredible moment for any Leicester
City supporter and your instinct is to go wild with delight. But you're working.
You're in the press box. You face a dilemma.

Or not.

'All semblance of journalistic impartiality went out the window,' says James
Sharpe of the *Leicester Mercury*. 'I was up, arms in the air, jumping around like a
maniac.

'I'm better now. You'd think that this season, being top of the table, I'd be even
worse. But I've been quite reserved recently. I think it's because Leicester are so defensively sound, they never inspire nerves in the fans. It's still all very scary, though.
Don't look down, eh?'

Sharpe started working at the *Mercury* in September 2012. His first season ended,
along with City's dreams of promotion, at Vicarage Road.

'God, that was horrendous,' he says. 'I might even have shed the odd tear when I
got back to the car. I wasn't doing every City game at that stage, but did cover that
one as well as the victory at Nottingham Forest.

'I've never found it hard to be objective in my writing. I've always been the sort
of fan who would analyse performances and pick out the good and bad. I've rarely
been one to see things through blue-tinted spectacles. It's the same with my writing.
It means I can be passionate but not biased, and I think that's a good combination.'

This season has been incredibly different to the one it followed in many respects
but one of the main changes for the media has been the nature of the club's press
conferences following the arrival of Claudio Ranieri to replace Nigel Pearson.

'I had a lot of time for Pearson,' says Sharpe. 'He did so much good for the club,
which should never be ignored.

'But the image he projected was a strange one. Behind closed doors, he was funny
and charming. I had a one-to-one with him at the training ground and he was
brilliant: articulate, making jokes. He even called me 'mate' twice. The day after a
match, he was completely the opposite. Another journalist even came up to me to
ask why we didn't get on.'

Ranieri approaches media relations from another perspective.

'Claudio is lovely, respectful and shakes everyone by the hand at press conferences. You can ask him anything and he's happy to answer. He gives you quirky lines

that make great back-page stories. He's an absolute dream.

'Even bog-standard questions about half-time substitutions, he won't hesitate to tell you the tactics behind why he made the changes. If you did that with Pearson, he would often just reply: 'because I wanted to' as though you were trying to trip him up.'

At what point did Sharpe begin to think this wasn't just an ordinary season? At what stage did he consider City were in a title race?

'It's never an ordinary season with Leicester City,' he says. 'No matter which end of the table it is.

'The first time I wrote that City were title contenders was after they went two points clear at the top with a win at Swansea in December.

'But the victory at Manchester City was huge. That was the moment when it turned from a bit of fun, sitting in the big boys' seat where you knew you didn't quite belong, to proving, hey, this side could win a title. They didn't just beat Manchester City, the team that many thought would coast to the title, but dismantled them. On their own turf.'

That win at the Etihad sent a strong signal to any remaining doubters, but it isn't the game Sharpe picks as the one where he wished he was back among the City supporters.

'I have seen every game this season, home and away,' he says. 'I would have loved to be in with the fans after the Crystal Palace win when they stood and sang for twenty minutes after the final whistle. That was special.

'The only other time I will wish to be in with the fans is if, and I will keep saying if, they go on to win it. I would love to be in with the fans when Big Wes, who has been such a rock and leader, lifts the trophy. I wish I could be able just to stand there and enjoy the moment, instead of having to spare a few thoughts for getting on with my work.

'But I can't complain. It's the best job in the world.'

34: WEST HAM UNITED (H)

Sunday 17 April 2016

WHEN WE MAKE THE PILGRIMAGE DOWN RAW DYKES ROAD FROM the city centre end, past the student accommodation and abandoned wasteland of Filbert Street to our left and the banks of the river Soar to our right, we are presented with a view of our football club's home and one of the first things we see is a hashtag.

Emblazoned on the outside of the King Power Stadium, it stands out like a sore thumb – a digital imprint on a physical world. Filbert Street, a place that was important to thousands of people, has been left to rot just yards away. When it was demolished, we lost not only a football ground but the graffiti that supporters daubed on its walls. The only graffiti there now refers to Israel and a couple of Polish football clubs.

We marked Filbert Street as our territory over the decades, something that is unimaginable at the King Power Stadium where the stamp is official and comes as part of a marketing strategy.

Whether you see that as a sign of progress from the days of petty vandalism or a sad indictment of modern corporate precedence, it's there and you can't miss it.

And after the hashtag, it reads: Fearless.

Like a well-known yeast extract product, it splits opinion. Some fans love it. Some hate it. Either way, there's definitely some truth to it. This team has consistently shown attitude and belief and they don't seem to worry about any opponent.

Supporters, on the other hand, are free to fear anyone and everyone. Today we fear Andy Carroll and Dimitri Payet, two West Ham United attackers who could barely be any more different from one another.

In Carroll's case, a single performance made waves – a hat-trick in a barnstorming display in the previous Saturday's 3-3 home draw with Arsenal. He was a force of nature that day, desperately climbing high above the Arsenal defenders like a father who has bet a million pounds that he can score a goal against his young children.

Payet, meanwhile, has been one of the Premier League's classiest performers all season thanks to his superlative first touch, close control and creativity. He is also the best set piece taker in the country, perhaps Europe, perhaps the world. A recent free kick against Crystal Palace flew into the top corner at such startling pace that it seemed to re-define what was possible from the strike of a ball.

So we're scared. Some of us.

Others take a look at the league table and wonder what the fuss is all about. Leicester City go into the clash with West Ham a full twenty points ahead of the visitors. We should have so much confidence in our team. We've lost three games out of 33 this season. Believe. Come on. Believe in this team.

We have to enjoy this. We won't ever experience it again. Not like this.

Besides, the fear may manifest itself in concern at our team facing individuals like Carroll and Payet but our team – let's remember – is brilliant. The fear doesn't come from this team's failures. It's the ones from the past – the FA Cup quarter-final defeat to Wycombe Wanderers in 2001; the 4-1 home loss against Sheffield Wednesday in 2008 when everything went so very wrong so very quickly; David Speedie; Steve White and Paul Bodin; Troy Deeney, Troy bloody Deeney – these are the ghosts that bring on the fear.

These next few weeks will be scary not because it's West Ham or Swansea or even Manchester United but because of how much this means. We should be having the time of our lives – and, again, some are, and they can't fathom how anybody isn't enjoying this – yet many supporters just want it to be over now. They can't take any more, especially when plenty of people have decided the league has already been won.

It hasn't. This is Leicester City. Even Claudio Ranieri himself says as much in his pre-match press conference:

'Football is very strange. If you weren't here in Leicester but somewhere else, maybe [Manchester] City or United, with seven points more, you would say 'it is finished'.

'At this moment you don't think this. Why? Because we are Leicester. We have to fight and we have to be focused and strong.'

We're trying to be strong too, Claudio. We are.

When Liverpool were top of the league towards the end of the 2013/14 season, their fans would line the streets outside Anfield to welcome the team bus as it approached the stadium. Then came a Steven Gerrard slip and a Crystal Palace fightback. We're not replicating that, partly because our players all arrive separately two and half hours before kick-off. Our nod to the situation is a roar from behind the goal as the squad prepares to carry out the final pre-match drill in the south-west corner of the pitch. These are the things you notice – the small differences that mark today out as playing a significant part in the club's history.

This match will, like so many this season, take place twice. One match will be played out at the King Power Stadium with over thirty thousand in attendance. The other is shown on screens of all shapes and sizes across the globe. They're the same match, of course, but they're so very different.

One is emotional. It's alive. It's of the moment. It's viewed from one vantage point for ninety minutes. It's partisan. It's wanting one man wearing one coloured shirt to get to the ball before another man in another coloured shirt, over and over and over again. Put the ball in one net. Keep it out of the other. And hate the other team and hate the man in black and his little helpers on either side of the pitch. Hate them all for ninety minutes.

The other match isn't like that. The other match is cold. Rational. Slick. Just the first of two matches in today's Super Sunday extravaganza. It's intro, montage, analysis, montage, advertisements, montage until the go-ahead is given.

And then we play.

Same team as normal for us. They shuffle the pack after a tiring FA Cup quarter-final defeat to Manchester United in midweek. Payet starts, but Carroll is consigned to the substitutes' bench.

As the radio presenter Danny Baker often says, football is chaos. There are so many variables affected by so many actors that it can't be anything else. This game is the most chaotic of the season. It's completely mad from start to finish, both inside the stadium and on the television screens.

The madness starts in the first minute when a Payet free kick is headed towards goal by Cheikhou Kouyaté. Kasper Schmeichel leaps full length to his left and claws the ball onto the post. It then rolls along the goal line and touches the opposite post before deflecting back into Schmeichel's grasp. He looks as relieved as we are. Only eighty-nine minutes of this to go. Plus injury time.

In match one – inside the stadium – this is the kind of thing that stops hearts.

In match two – on television – West Ham are unlucky not to be ahead. It's not physics or basic cause and effect that took the ball onto both posts. It's luck.

West Ham look good. Thankfully, we are at our most dangerous when the other team is playing well. City stopped scoring from counter attacks for a short time while opposition teams spent the entire game guarding patiently against them. West Ham are here to attack, which makes them vulnerable.

Schmeichel claims a cross and sends the ball forward to Riyad Mahrez. In match one, it doesn't register that our goalkeeper has set up the attack with inch-perfect distribution. We notice every time he kicks it straight out of play, of course.

Mahrez takes three touches before directing a measured pass between two West Ham players to the onrushing N'Golo Kanté.

Match one: the West Ham defence is opening up. Kanté can run clear through on goal and score. Why's he passing it out to the left?

Match two: the best decision Kanté can make, a precise through ball to our top goalscorer.

Jamie Vardy collects the ball and strikes it across Adrian in the West Ham goal with his left foot into the far corner of the net. Match one: elation. Match two: the latest chapter in the fairy tale.

This isn't a fairy tale though. This is real life. This isn't cold and rational and slick. It's emotional. It's chaos. It's about to all go horribly wrong, just like it always does eventually.

The worst thing is how quickly it happens. One moment, Danny Drinkwater is playing a through ball for Vardy to chase into the penalty area. The next, Jonathan Moss is producing a red card and City's 22-goal star striker is leaving the pitch.

Match one: penalty! He's blowing his whistle and racing towards the area! Wait. Oh no. Oh no, no, no. He's booking him for diving. Oh God, no. Ten men. For half an hour. With a one goal lead. And no Vardy. And no Vardy for Swansea, either. Oh no, no, no, no, no. 132 years without a league title and this is the closest we're ever going to get because Jonathan Moss – yes, him, who lost his head and made one of the worst refereeing decisions in City's recent history by sending off Kasper Schmeichel at the City Ground five years ago – has done it again. He's done it to us again.

Match two: through gritted teeth, probably the correct decision. Or at least understandable.

Here comes the Alamo.

West Ham start launching the ball up to Andy Carroll, who came on at half time.

Match one: time passes so very, very slowly.

Match two: time passes at the same pace it always does.

We tick off the minutes one by one until there are less than ten left, plus injury time.

Then it happens.

Match one: the ball comes across, Leonardo Ulloa makes the clearance and we can release another sigh of relief. Wait. What? He's given a penalty. He's given a bloody penalty.

Match two: something to do with warning Wes Morgan and Robert Huth about holding or blocking opposition players in the penalty area on numerous occasions.

Match one: none of that matters. This referee wants to stop us winning the league for the first time in our 132-year history. This ref.

Carroll – of course – strokes the ball into the net.

Most fans are incandescent with rage. Some are crying. One can't take it any longer. He sets off down the stairs from SK1 and walks the length of the East Stand concourse. When he gets to the end, he hears a muffled roar from above and he knows what has happened.

Match two: Aaron Cresswell sends a dipping volley beyond Schmeichel into the net. West Ham lead 2-1.

Match one: back to SK1, emotionally broken by a ridiculous game of a ridiculous sport.

Match two: West Ham are back in the Champions League hunt. Tottenham Hotspur are back in the title race. Leicester City are on the floor.

This is what we feared, but there is one final twist.

With seconds remaining, Jeff Schlupp drives into the opposition penalty area and Carroll moves across to block him off.

Match one: just laughter. He's given it.

Match two: he's evened it up.

Penalty. Ulloa sticks it away and it's 2-2. The belief has been restored. No matter who or what gets in this team's way, they find an answer. We cheer our players. We boo the referee. And we wait to see if Stoke City – beautiful, beautiful Stoke City; our favourite team in all the land, this week – can do us a favour and get a result at home to Tottenham on Monday evening.

Three hours before kick-off at the Britannia Stadium, the FA charges Jamie Vardy with improper conduct. A recent precedent saw Chelsea's Diego Costa banned for an extra match, meaning we are beginning to think about the prospect of visiting Old Trafford without the 22-goal striker who has terrorised Manchester United twice in the past two years.

The spotlight on the club at this time is beyond anything we've ever known. This is the price of success.

So we rely on Stoke to lift our spirits, which they comprehensively fail to do. Harry Kane scores the opening goal for Tottenham inside the first ten minutes and his team strolls to a 4-0 win. We're going to have to do this the hard way.

We're five points clear at the top of the Premier League with four games to go. We'll be back on Sunday and we'll be loud.

Leicester City 2 (Vardy, Ulloa)
West Ham United 2 (Carroll, Cresswell)
Team: Schmeichel, Simpson, Morgan, Huth, Fuchs, Mahrez (Amartey), Drinkwater, Kanté, Albrighton (Schlupp), Okazaki (Ulloa), Vardy

THE NUMBER 23

LEONARDO ULLOA STANDS IN FRONT OF THE LEICESTER CITY fans celebrating a vital last minute equaliser against West Ham United and howls. His neck muscles are tensed. His veins bulge. And we love him.

It's easy to forget that Ulloa was, at first, an unpopular signing. The transfer deal took weeks to complete and many supporters were underwhelmed by his eventual arrival. City paid Brighton and Hove Albion a record fee to bring Ulloa to the King Power in the summer of 2015, creating a burden of expectation.

Fans were overly influenced by his final two games for Brighton in a televised two-legged play-off semi-final against Derby County. Ulloa was poor in those games, perhaps as a result of injury or fatigue – a shadow of the player who scored twice against City just a few weeks earlier and impressed our centre-backs to such a degree that they recommended his signing.

Some backed Ulloa, feeling his strength and aerial ability would perfectly complement Jamie Vardy's pace and energy. In fact, it was the pairing of Ulloa and Vardy that appeared to stunt City's progress in the 2014/15 season as David Nugent's relentless work rate was sorely missed. It took several months for the combination to finally flourish when Nigel Pearson changed the formation to 3-5-2 and restore control of the midfield.

Ulloa's personal form mirrored that of the team – an impressive start, during which he scored five goals in five games, followed by a mid-season slump and then vital early openers against Swansea City and Newcastle United to help make the great escape possible. Those ups and downs masked the fact he had been an overall success – the top goalscorer in a side that beat the odds to stave off the threat of relegation, all in his first season in the Premier League.

The upheaval in the summer that followed meant an uncertain future for Ulloa. Was there a place for him in an attacking setup that relied heavily on the energetic style of Vardy and Shinji Okazaki? Could he press opposition defenders effectively? Would he be able to participate in the lightning counter-attacks that were becoming synonymous with City's approach?

While not emphatic, the answers proved to be positive in the long run. Ulloa refreshed his role in the squad, playing a key role in two of the most impressive performances of the season at Newcastle and Swansea – the same two sides he had terrorised towards the end of the previous campaign – and then reverted to the role of second-half substitute to great effect. His late winner against Norwich restored belief after the cruel nature of defeat at the Emirates. His hold-up play deep into the second half was crucial as City clung onto 1-0 advantages throughout March.

Through it all, he kept smiling.

He saved a precious point against West Ham and Jamie Vardy's suspension means that he will be called upon from the start seven days later.

Leonardo Ulloa, your time is now.

35: SWANSEA CITY (H)

Sunday 24 April 2016

ST PETER'S BASILICA IN VATICAN CITY, CLOSE TO WHERE Claudio Ranieri grew up in Rome, is one of the largest churches in the world and a place of pilgrimage for millions of visitors each year. Inside, a sign excluding tourists from one of its chapels of worship reads:

INGRESSO RISERVATO AI FEDELI CHE PARTECIPANO ALLA CELEBRAZIONE

Beneath those words, there is an English translation:

ENTRY RESERVED TO THE BELIEVERS INVOLVED IN CELEBRATION

At 9.00am on Thursday 21 April, tickets for away supporters go on sale for the last match of the season at Stamford Bridge. They're sold out within hours. That's the entry part sorted. But do we believe? And will we be celebrating?

The maelstrom of the West Ham game is still fresh in our minds as we wake up the following Sunday and contemplate the enormity of the afternoon ahead. The hands on the clock seem to stand still. What kind of kick-off time is 4.15pm anyway?

We need today to be one of those great escape games: like Newcastle, when we were 2-0 up inside seventeen minutes; like Southampton, when we were 2-0 up inside nineteen minutes. It's quite a coincidence how the same fixtures have fallen twelve months later. Newcastle and Southampton have both been defeated again and now Swansea are back in town.

It was Leonardo Ulloa whose opener helped to put the Swans to the sword last April. Almost a year to the day, Ulloa is charged with leading the line in place of the suspended Jamie Vardy and there is huge pressure on the Argentine to deliver. Claudio Ranieri makes one other change: Jeff Schlupp is in to add pace and power to the left wing in place of Marc Albrighton.

These players have earned the right to be trusted, regardless of Vardy's absence. They have answered every question all season. Forget West Ham. Forget Jonathan Moss. Forget Tottenham. Just win. However it happens. Whatever it takes. Don't just answer the critics. Answer us, the nervous amongst us.

A tifo helps to calm those nerves. This is the fourth of the large-scale displays to be organised by Union FS. A couple of giant banners held aloft across the middle of the Kop read: 'History makes us who we are'. We wave blue and white flags and we wait for our team to answer our plea.

Thankfully, our team is absolutely bloody brilliant. All season, they've been brilliant. In this game, they're brilliant. And it is like one of the games from the great escape.

Riyad Mahrez, within hours of being named PFA Footballer of the Year, scores the first goal after a mistake by Swansea captain Ashley Williams. Mahrez slides on his knees in front of L1 as he did on the opening day of the season after scoring a penalty against Sunderland, but his expression is different this time. No big smile. This is serious business. Ranieri himself said it in his pre-match press conference – now we're going for the title.

Mahrez has stepped up. Now it's Ulloa's turn. First he nods a Danny Drinkwater free kick into the net at the near post and then, after half time, he shows great belief and determination to slide the ball in from close range following Schlupp's powerful burst down the left.

The rare luxury of a 3-0 lead with plenty of time left to enjoy football again. It's been a while. None of this 1-0 nonsense. None of this clinging on in the last five minutes. None of this dependency on refereeing decisions. Just a win, as we requested, one of the easiest of the season at the best possible time. We even give our players the 'olé' treatment, hilariously, during a game in which our team has surrendered possession in trademark fashion. City still have twice as many shots as Swansea and nine times as many shots on target.

The fourth goal involves all three substitutes: the frightening pace of Demarai Gray, who runs with the ball three-quarters of the length of the pitch; the mis-placed header by Andy King; the finish from Marc Albrighton.

'4-0 to the one-man team,' we sing. That man, Jamie Vardy, applauds from an executive box as all ten outfield players congregate in celebration of Albrighton's goal.

'Barcelona, we're coming for you,' we sing. They're not all that.

'Are you watching Tottenham?' we sing. They're good, but they're not as good as us.

'We're gonna win the league,' we sing. That league, that win, is so close now.

This is the strange thing: despite all the noise, the goals, the atmosphere, there is something bizarrely low-key about it all. It feels routine, like the kind of performance we know this team is capable of producing. Even when the pressure is on and the entire world is watching, this team can achieve great things.

This team stands on the edge of history.

Leicester City 4 (Mahrez, Ulloa 2, Albrighton)
Swansea City 0
Team: Schmeichel, Simpson, Morgan, Huth, Fuchs, Mahrez, Drinkwater, Kanté, Schlupp (Albrighton), Okazaki (Gray), Ulloa (King)

THE PLAYER

FRAN GAMBLE IS A PASSIONATE LEICESTER CITY FAN. AND she plays for Tottenham Hotspur.

'I got my first Leicester shirt when I was seven or eight and it still fits me, which I'm quite impressed about,' she laughs. 'There was a time when I considered supporting Liverpool but my dad threatened to throw me out. So it was Leicester. I liked Steve Guppy because I played on the left wing too.

'I had a season playing for Forest. I'm not proud of that. I didn't enjoy putting the shirt on at all.'

Geography has taken Gamble south to London where she lives and works as a teacher. The nearest team was Tottenham, where she has played for several seasons. She now turns out for Spurs reserves, currently involved in a title race of their own with Brighton and Hove Albion.

'Once you get out on the pitch, it's so much easier being a player than being a supporter,' she says. 'You can dictate what happens. As a fan you put all of your hopes in the hands of the players. Following it is far, far more stressful. I've had sleepless nights about Leicester this season.

'During the West Ham game, I actually had my Tottenham kit on because we were playing against Lewes Ladies at the same time. It was a good distraction. I end up pacing round my flat or trying to distract myself otherwise. I'll be messaging my mum back in Leicester.

'While I was playing, I kept asking about the score and someone told me Vardy had been sent off. I didn't want to believe them. I thought they were winding me up.'

There must have been a lot of that this season, living in north London surrounded by supporters of title rivals?

'Quite a few of my team-mates are Tottenham fans. We have a WhatsApp group. There are Arsenal fans too and they were lively after the game at the Emirates this season. My reply was 'just you wait until Chelsea give us a guard of honour at Stamford Bridge on the last day', which was tongue-in-cheek at the time.'

Now it could happen.

'I have a permanent grin on my face at the moment. I go into school and parents come up to me in the playground talking to me about Leicester. The kids assumed I'd just been supporting them this season so I took in my old Leicester shirt as proof.'

The idea that any City fan could be accused of being a glory hunter would have been unthinkable until the past few months.

'I don't think there are words to describe it,' says Gamble. 'It's unreal. League One seems such a short time ago and we've made this jump. It's ridiculous.'

In addition to her teaching role, Gamble is also the head coach of the England Under 18 Independent Schools side. She arrived at the England team's training centre at St George's Park in Burton-on-Trent one chilly morning in December to coach her team against a Welsh college.

'It was the day after Leicester had played Chelsea,' she says. 'I got out of my car and the first person I saw was Mark Clattenburg, who had refereed that game. Straight away I asked him how many minutes of injury time he had played. He said he had been enjoying the game. I told him it stressed me out!'

The stress levels reach an all-time high towards the end of the Monday night game between Tottenham and West Bromwich Albion.

Tottenham have been brilliant this season. They play admirable, possession-based football and they have youth on their side. Harry Kane, Dele Alli, Toby Alderweireld, Hugo Lloris: they've all been exceptional.

We say this through gritted teeth, of course. Some of us don't admit it at all. It's us against them. Even Fran Gamble in her Tottenham shirt: she is desperate for Tottenham to lose.

They keep winning though. In fact, they lost only one of the fourteen games that followed Robert Huth's winner at White Hart Lane in January. Straight after City's win at Sunderland, Tottenham beat Manchester United 3-0. The night after Vardy's sending-off and two dropped points against West Ham, they thrashed Stoke City 4-0 at the Britannia Stadium.

Now City have also won 4-0 and Tottenham must respond again.

Monday 25 April. White Hart Lane. The West Bromwich Albion defender Craig Dawson scores for Tottenham Hotspur in the first half and scores for West Bromwich Albion in the second half. He may as well not have bothered scoring at all. Tottenham need a goal in the dying minutes.

It doesn't sound like the King Power does when we need a goal. The Spurs fans are not roaring their team on. They are nervous. They are worried. They are quiet. And the goal isn't coming. Miraculously, it isn't coming.

The final whistle is blown. This is the night where Tottenham Hotspur's title challenge takes the penultimate blow. One last punch – one win for City or one defeat for Spurs – will finish it once and for all.

We have obsessed over the gap between first and second place for months and now it stands at seven points with just three games remaining. Leicester City need three points from those last three games to win the Premier League title.

Old Trafford. King Power Stadium. Stamford Bridge.

Manchester United. Everton. Chelsea.

Three points.

So close.

'I had the feeling from when Spurs hit the post twice,' says Gamble. 'I thought this was going to be it. When West Brom scored, I said to my mum it was too early. When the final whistle went, that was the first time I allowed myself to believe a little bit but now I've gone back to being apprehensive about it all.

'My phone went mad on Monday night with Spurs mates telling me we've done it.

'But this is Leicester. Never ever is it finished until it's mathematically done.'

It could be mathematically done before Tottenham play again. Leicester City have the chance to win the league at Old Trafford.

36: MANCHESTER UNITED (A)

Sunday 1 May 2016

IT'S THE BIGGEST GAME IN LEICESTER CITY FOOTBALL CLUB'S history.

But that's all it is.

Only a game.

Five days before thousands of us travel north to Manchester, the jury gives its verdict following the two-year inquest into the deaths of 96 Liverpool supporters at their team's FA Cup semi-final at Hillsborough on 15 April 1989.

96 people died. They left home to watch their football team and never came back.

The jury finds there was no behaviour on the part of football supporters which caused or contributed to the dangerous situation at the Leppings Lane turnstiles. The formality of the language contrasts starkly with the stories published following the verdict.

Those stories are horrifying but I force myself to read them because the truth – the real truth, the truth many people concealed or denied for decades – is far too important to evade.

I don't remember the Hillsborough disaster. It happened just months before I started going to football matches.

I went to my first away game in March 1991: Notts County v Leicester City at Meadow Lane. I was six years old, standing in one of the pens on the terracing with my dad. The away end was packed so a gate was opened to allow supporters into the stand along one side of the ground. Fans surged through and I was pushed towards the front of the pen, separated from my dad. A family managed to offer some protection but when my dad eventually found me, he discovered that I had wire mesh imprinted on one cheek after the surge of the crowd pressed me against the metal fencing.

Nobody was seriously hurt. Some fans suffered minor injuries. Perhaps it wasn't that scary for most people but, as a six-year-old, the panic I felt at being separated from my dad is one of my earliest memories.

When I got home, I told him I never wanted to go to another away game.

As I prepare for the trip to Old Trafford twenty-five years later, the eighteenth and penultimate league away game of the season, I talk to my mum about Hillsborough.

'If that had been you, I would have been devastated,' she says. 'But imagine if they'd then said it was your fault.'

I see the same people standing in the away end in Manchester that I saw at Hereford and Yeovil less than ten years earlier, people who have become friends over the years. I can't help thinking about those supporters who left home in 1989 and never came back.

Only a game.

A banner stretching out across the Sir Alex Ferguson Stand is a reminder of what's at stake for our football club: The Impossible Dream.

City are unchanged, still without the suspended Jamie Vardy, and Manchester United start like they've only got ten minutes to score as many goals as possible. They manage one. Our boys are clinging on and Kasper Schmeichel pulls off a wonderful save to ensure the deficit isn't doubled.

Within minutes, that deficit is instead wiped out. Danny Drinkwater lofts a free kick into the penalty area and Wes Morgan heads the ball past David De Gea in the United goal. We're back in it and we're ecstatic.

It's a pulsating game. City are forced to retreat by waves of United pressure. The defence holds firm. Robert Huth pulls Marouane Fellaini's hair. Fellaini elbows Huth in the throat. The referee is oblivious. Danny Simpson's mistake lets Jesse Lingard in. Simpson recovers. Schmeichel clears.

City's attacking play improves in the second half and Leonardo Ulloa sends a couple of headers off target from set pieces, while Riyad Mahrez finds space on the counter attack as the pitch becomes stretched by both teams' thirst for victory.

There are no more goals, only a red card: Drinkwater shown a second yellow for a tug on United substitute Memphis Depay on the cusp of the penalty area.

City hold on. The game ends all square. Like at Selhurst and Sunderland, we stay and we sing about how we're going to win the league. Not today, but we're going to do it.

We're only a game away.

Only a game.

Seventeen-year-old City fan Samuel Garner watched the Manchester United game on television with his family in Leicester. Afterwards, he went into the city centre with his friends. He was walking along Welford Road when he was hit by a car. The driver failed to stop.

Samuel died at the scene wearing his white City shirt.

He didn't make it home.

Manchester United 1 (Martial)

Leicester City 1 (Morgan)

Team: Schmeichel, Simpson, Morgan, Huth, Fuchs, Mahrez (King), Drinkwater, Kanté, Schlupp (Albrighton), Okazaki (Gray), Ulloa

THE MAGICIAN

HERE'S RIYAD MAHREZ, THE ALGERIAN PRINCE. LOPING, THE trickster, the slippery fish. Cocking the snook. Giving defenders a hint of the ball but he's got it on a string and he yanks it back at the last moment and away he goes. Snaking into the box. Curving his approach like a high speed train on a slight bend. Living the dream of half a continent. The darling of a digital invasion, all heart shapes and exclamation marks. They love him even more than we do, the Algerians. They take over Facebook with their love for their hero.

The best player of Leicester! Mahrez the greatest! Algeria loves Leicester City!

Mahrez is the jewel in this Leicester City team. He's the one that makes things happen. Everything is geared towards getting him the ball in space and everything else is plan B.

Some fans get frustrated when things don't quite come off for Mahrez, when the tricks don't work and possession is lost. They miss the point. No creative player is absolutely perfect. You need players who take risks.

Thankfully, this is the season when everything is going right for Riyad Mahrez.

Finishing never used to be his strong point. He would wind his way past a defender or two, get to the edge of the box and stroke a tame effort straight at the opposition goalkeeper. There was so much potential there but how did you fit it into a successful football team? Someone who could beat players for fun but didn't always have the end product: was there a place at all?

This season has been different. At times, Mahrez has done the opposite. He struggled throughout the home game against Aston Villa but he still delivered the corner that brought the first goal, constructed one of his trademark dribbles past numerous opponents to help create the equaliser and then laid on the winner with a delicate chip into the penalty area.

Even during a low-key first half, he managed to put three Villa defenders on their backsides with one deft turn on the edge of the box.

That goes viral.

It's uploaded time after time and liked and shared and retweeted for days. This mercurial Algerian is a twenty-first century superstar, appealing to millions worldwide with his stylish approach to the beautiful game, and social media loves him.

Mahrez the magician: a player who brings supporters out of their seats when he gets the ball and heads towards goal. He's humiliated countless opponents, often two or three at a time.

He's one of the greatest we've ever seen.

PFA Footballer of the Year 2015/16: Riyad Mahrez.

36 AND A HALF:
CHELSEA V TOTTENHAM HOTSPUR

Monday 2 May 2016

WE'VE BEEN SINGING ABOUT STAMFORD BRIDGE FOR A FEW weeks now, asking the Chelsea fans whether they're listening and telling them to keep the trophy glistening because we're coming in May to take it away. Before that, we could do with a small favour.

The second opportunity for Leicester City to win the Premier League arrives on Bank Holiday Monday with Tottenham Hotspur's trip to west London.

For one night only, we're all Chelsea fans.

Our players gather at Jamie Vardy's house in Melton Mowbray to watch the game.

Ian Stringer will report live from Stamford Bridge for BBC Radio Leicester, the slight delay in radio and television broadcasts meaning he will know before anyone else whether the title has been confirmed.

The rest of us will watch and wait.

Some of us watching in pubs: Warren Nolan the closest to the action, proudly wearing his City shirt in the Chelsea Potter on the King's Road; Chloe Dexter and her friend Mike at the Soar Point in Leicester; Liam Finn with his stepdad at the Albion Sports Bar in Earl Shilton; Roy Harteveld at the Bricklayers Arms in the village of Laxton in East Yorkshire, planning to turn a minute-long walk home into a half-hour stagger; Jason Becker one of several stateside City fans at the Football Factory in New York.

Some of us trying not to wake or alarm young children: Chris Tadman in Syston, having endured his two-year-old son Olly singing about Leonardo Ulloa at the top of his voice all the way from Llandudno earlier in the day; Alex Malpass in Hinckley with his ten-week-old son Oscar, his dog that looks like a piglet and several cans of Skol.

Some of us watching at home: Kate Morrissey heading to her mum Ann Lawrence's house in Grantham; Alex Marsh in Berkhamsted with his girlfriend Vicki and a thirteen-week foetus with the working title N'Golo; Chris Rice from underneath a pile of boxes in Lincoln as he prepares to move house; Sunil and Hitesh Parmar in Bedford with their dad; Jonny Cox in Leicester with his dog Alfie; Glenn Worth on his sofa in Narborough; Karl Peutrill from behind his sofa in St Albans.

Some who can't bear to watch it any more: Raj Kumar, listening to Radio Five at home in Leicester.

And spare a thought for Will Parsons, surreptitiously checking his phone for updates during a performance of The Lion King at the Lyceum Theatre in London.

Thousands more across the world. Wherever we are, we've been on tenterhooks for weeks. Months. Years. Will it happen tonight?

The game kicks off and the tension kicks in. Chelsea are up for it but Tottenham look worryingly dangerous on the break, spreading play left and right to their marauding full-backs Danny Rose and Kyle Walker while their four attackers interchange fluidly.

Every time Chelsea go forward, we rise a little from our seats. There's a chance for Cesc Fàbregas but the Spaniard places his shot just wide of the far post. The atmosphere inside Stamford Bridge is stupendous. The action on the pitch isn't quite measuring up. Yet.

With thirty-three minutes gone, the ball is played behind the Chelsea defence and Harry Kane is through on goal. We remain calm. He must be offside. Kane takes the ball around Blues goalkeeper Asmir Begovic. No flag. Passes it into the empty net. Still no flag. Celebrates wildly in front of the Tottenham fans packed into the Shed End. Incredibly, still no flag. 1-0 Tottenham.

He had to be offside. Replay. Clearly onside. The nerves have gone now, replaced by dread.

It's okay. We're just going to have to do it ourselves. Trust in our players. They'll be watching this at Jamie Vardy's house and plotting Everton's downfall. Who will be the hero? Vardy? Riyad Mahrez? Andy King? Believe in them and their ability to respond.

Tottenham are rampant now, equally threatening in possession and on the counter attack, while the home side's composure disappears. Mauricio Pochettino's players are clearly trying to rile the combustible Diego Costa and it's working.

Another Spurs through ball sends Heung-Min Son clear in the right channel and the ball again ends up in Begovic's net. Son runs behind the goal to the jubilant Tottenham supporters.

This is gut-wrenching. It isn't that we don't trust our players to finish the job in the final two games of the season. The problem is that some of us were convinced it would happen tonight. We were certain Chelsea would put an end to this stress and allow Saturday to become the greatest party the city of Leicester has ever known. But no. Tottenham lead 2-0 at half time.

After Chelsea's previous game at Bournemouth, Eden Hazard was interviewed on Match of the Day. 'We don't want - the fans, the club, the players - Tottenham to win the Premier League,' Hazard said. 'We hope for Leicester because they deserve to be champions this season.'

Pedro is substituted and Hazard trots onto the pitch for the second half. Let's see how much you don't want Tottenham to win the league, Eden. Let's see how much you want this to happen for us.

Both the match and the atmosphere become increasingly hostile. Diego Costa, even more than normal, is a red card waiting to happen. Everyone is a red card waiting to happen.

Chelsea win a corner, which Willian delivers into the area. Gary Cahill escapes his marker to control the ball with his first touch and lash it into the net with his second. A roar. A huge roar. At Stamford Bridge. In the Chelsea Potter on the King's Road. All across Leicester. All across Leicestershire. In a grand house in Melton Mowbray. In a detached bungalow in Grantham. In the Bricklayers Arms in Laxton. From beneath a pile of boxes in Lincoln. From a sofa in Narborough. From behind a sofa in St Albans.

Minutes tick by. Time is running out for Chelsea. Time is running out, this evening at least, for Leicester City.

'We hope for Leicester because they deserve to be champions this season...'

There are 83 minutes on the clock when Eden Hazard collects the ball inside his own half and tricks his way past two opponents. He glides past a third, looking every inch the PFA Footballer of the Year of the previous season, checks back and passes to Diego Costa.

'We hope for Leicester…'

Costa moves past Toby Alderweireld on the edge of the box and slips a return pass into the path of Hazard.

'We hope…'

Hazard takes it first time on the instep of his right foot. The angle of the television camera is perfect. The ball starts off heading wide of the post but it's bending inwards. Hugo Lloris is at full stretch, just as he was when Riyad Mahrez's shot rocketed past him back in August to equalise at the King Power. It's bending inwards. We're off our seats now. It's bending inwards. Lloris is beaten. We're on our feet now. It's in.

And the noise. The most guttural noise. The most unearthly noise. A scream or a shriek or both.

It's in, and Leicester City are perhaps ten minutes away from the Premier League title.

We hope.

Settle down. Still time for Tottenham to find a winner. Still time for one of the men in white to ruin the party.

The thing is: it's not happening. It's pretty clear it's not happening for Tottenham tonight and it's not happening for Tottenham this season. They still have the bitter consolation prize of a Champions League place and the chance to finish above Arsenal for the first time in 21 years but there will be no first title since 1961.

It's not happening because they've lost their heads. Plenty said this would happen to us, that the pressure would get to our players and our title bid would go up in smoke. Even when the dark moment came, Jamie Vardy was sent off and two points were dropped against West Ham, this incredible set of players responded: 4-0 to the one-man team.

Some other responses this season: the early-season comebacks – Tottenham, Aston Villa, Stoke, Southampton; losing at Anfield and the defiant goalless draw against Manchester City three days later; the pair of Arsenal defeats and the long unbeaten runs that followed; Leonardo Ulloa's last-gasp equaliser against the Hammers.

We've got bottle. What have you got, Tottenham?

Stamford Bridge hums with anticipation as though Chelsea are about to be crowned champions of England. In fact, they are seconds away from losing that crown and their fans could not look happier. They sing about their former manager Claudio Ranieri. They sing about Leicester.

Deep into injury time, Willian stands over a free kick with a chance to win the game. Instead, he plays the ball out to the left to waste time and a manic laugh escapes: the audacity of it.

Hazard, the man who will never have to buy a drink in Leicester again, has the ball at his feet as Mark Clattenburg blows the final whistle, bringing 90 minutes to an end.

Bringing 132 years to an end.

Leicester City are the champions of England.

Chelsea 2 (Cahill, Hazard)
Tottenham Hotspur 2 (Kane, Son)

THE CITY UNITED

SIMON MCCARTHY AND TOM MOORE ARE TWO OF THOUSANDS who travel with City home and away, who became hooked during the O'Neill years and have experienced the club's greatest highs and lows in the past two decades.

They are also two of thousands who watched the battle of Stamford Bridge in pubs across Leicester city centre.

'The feeling in the pub at half time with Chelsea two goals down was strange,' says Simon. 'Before the game it seemed everyone was convinced Spurs would drop points. We were starting to think about the Everton game and you could feel a few nerves start to creep back in.'

'I was pretty relaxed,' says Tom. 'I was resigned to waiting until Saturday anyway. This team has never given me any reason not to trust and have complete faith in them.'

When Gary Cahill scored to halve the deficit, he put Leicester City within a goal of glory.

'Spurs were rattled and every City chant in the pub was belted out twice as loud,' says Tom. 'It felt as if we were in the home end ourselves sucking the ball into the goal. You really could feel the equaliser coming.'

That equaliser came when Hazard exchanged passes with Diego Costa and curled the ball into the top corner.

'As soon as Hazard scored everyone knew that was it,' says Simon. 'Tottenham were shot.

'The full time whistle went and it was just bedlam across the pub, front to back. No care for anything else in the world, just living in that moment. The combination of the noise of pint glasses shattering and my mates and I going wild will live with me forever.

'We were together when we got relegated to League One eight years earlier and we were together to see us become champions of England. I wouldn't even know these people if it wasn't for Leicester City and here I was sharing possibly the greatest experience of my life with them.'

'I'd have wanted it no other way,' agrees Tom. 'I must have hugged everyone at least five times each.

'On the way to the bar I passed some of the coaching team. The party was in full flow for those guys. I made sure I thanked them for helping to make this happen.'

'After it all died down I tried to take it in,' says Simon. 'But then I turned around to see Matt Reeves, Dave Rennie and the rest of the sports science team downing WKD's. How fantastic to share that moment with some of the people who made it all possible. Matt Reeves somehow managed to head-butt a lamp hanging from the ceiling.'

No wonder the club published a photograph on social media the following morning of a sign declaring the training ground's treatment room closed due to 'unforeseen circumstances'.

'I knew there'd be a bit of a gathering around the Market Tavern so a few of us headed into town armed with champagne,' says Tom.

'The walk from the pub up past the university building is usually a quiet one, but not that night. I don't think a car entered the city without hammering its horn.

'We were running, skipping and chanting at every car, high-fiving drivers and passengers. The scenes were something I could never have imagined.

'It was gridlock but we somehow forced our way into the huge crowd outside the Market Tavern, where there was a huge street party.

'After bouncing through what seemed like our entire songbook I managed to negotiate a bit of space and went for a proper spray with the champagne – a top-of-the-world feeling.

'Then we went up to the Clock Tower. There were people climbing up it. That felt like a carnival with younger fans and students getting involved.'

Even having witnessed scenes like this, the magnitude of Leicester City's achievement may never sink in for some supporters. The sense of wonder takes us back to where our passion for the club first took hold.

'My first game was Blackburn at Filbert Street under the lights in late December 1998,' says Simon. 'I remember it like it was yesterday, being pitch side and having my photo taken with Filbert the Fox. At that point I knew I was hooked.'

'It became my life from 2004 onwards,' says Tom. 'I was there every week from Plymouth to Carlisle, despite us being, at times, almost unwatchable. It was a real adventure.

'Having watched us lose 6-1 in the rain at Portsmouth on a Friday night makes these incredible moments even more special.'

37: EVERTON (H)

Saturday 7 May 2016

YOU WAKE UP.

Today's the day.

It's too early.

Today's the day.

Too excited.

Today's the day.

Today's the day you see the captain of your football club lift the Premier League trophy.

You had planned a time to set off. You bring it forward a bit. You've got to be there. Maybe being there will help it to sink in. But probably not.

Along the way you see blue and white flags and scarves hanging from windows and suspended from buildings, growing in number as you get closer as though they're guiding you in.

And then, there it is. The home of the champions. The traffic slows to a crawl. Everyone wants to see this. There are still six and a half hours until kick off but the stadium looks like it normally does just before a match. The queue for the club shop snakes out of the door and winds its way through the crowds.

You drive on, you park up and you grin at the complete stranger parking his car next to yours. He grins back. No reason, other than: we are the champions of England. You and him and tens of thousands of people who never dreamt this could happen: we are the champions of England.

You walk to the pub. You've made this journey hundreds of times before but never like this. Never surrounded by people who haven't even got tickets but just want to be a part of it. There are so many Italians – you see the shirts and scarves of Roma, Napoli, Fiorentina, Catania, Pontevedra. They love Claudio. They love Leicester.

There are three City fans dressed as giant pizza slices heading in the direction of a group of Italians. It looks like a Japanese game show.

The pub is empty. Everyone is outside enjoying the first bright heat of summer. You meet friends and family. Since you last met these people, you all became champions. You smile and shake your head in disbelief. They do the same.

You set off for the ground. The chancers are out in force selling T-shirts: 'The Peoples Champions'. You tut at the missing apostrophes and walk on.

Thousands of people have gathered outside the stadium. This has never happened before. It's beautifully spontaneous. People just needing to be here. There are still three hours until kick off.

You see more friends. You swap stories of where you were when the league was won. What you did. How it felt. You walk through the crowds together.

Coaches arrive, mostly seeming to carry Thai schoolchildren. You roar them in as though they contain your team. One of them actually does contain the other team. Who are we playing again?

It doesn't matter any more. It happened. This could have been a hard luck story or a nearly men story but it's not because it happened. We actually did it.

Rain begins to fall. Time to head inside. You're clutching the same card you've been carrying in your wallet all season: the one that allows entry to the home of Leicester City. Over the past few months that card has turned into a badge of pride. Today it feels like the most coveted item in England. People are paying more for a single ticket to this match than you paid to see all nineteen home league games.

You're one of the lucky ones. You hold the card up to the reader, the light turns green and you're in. The concourse is full of songs and blue smoke bombs. You take a deep breath and push through the clouds and the crowds.

You climb the steps out of the concourse to gaze at the pitch. The ground staff have cut a tartan pattern into the turf. Everybody is rising to the occasion. It looks sensational, ready for the first home game of the season rather than the last.

It is the last though. Alan Birchenall, club ambassador and pre-match rabble rouser, is running round the pitch for charity as he has done at the last home game of the season for the past thirty-six years. This is usually the main event. Not today.

With half an hour to go until kick off, Claudio Ranieri leads the world-renowned opera singer Andrea Bocelli onto the pitch and the music strikes up: Nessun Dorma, the anthem of Italia '90.

There was a boy who turned six years old six days after the World Cup final in 1990. He had only just fallen in love with Leicester City. Football terrified him at Notts County a few months later. He had no idea that one day, football would also make him feel like this: like he was put on earth to live these moments.

As he waves his flag; as he looks up at the plane circling above, pulling a banner referencing a league win rather than demanding the departure of a manager or chairman; as Bocelli brings Nessun Dorma to its magnificent crescendo: he thinks to himself, it feels like I am about to die. It feels like this is a film and the script comes to a close at this exact moment. Not in a bad way. In the best way possible. It feels like this is it.

Then a new melody begins, the moment passes and Bocelli is into his second song. The big screen at the other end of the stadium shows a close-up of the Premier League trophy glistening in the early evening light, blue and gold ribbons on either side. Pride swells.

It's easy to forget but there's a game to be played. Everton, who arrived in one of those coaches hours ago, give a guard of honour to the new champions of England.

The team has an unfamiliar look following the suspensions of Robert Huth and Danny Drinkwater but our leading goalscorer is back: Schmeichel; Simpson, Morgan, Wasilewski, Fuchs; Mahrez, Kanté, King, Albrighton; Okazaki, Vardy.

The noise is incessant. The whole repertoire is out and one song gets an extended airing:

Leicester boys are we, pride of our city,

In good times and in bad, we always back the lads,

We're gonna win the league.

We already have, but this team is relentless. They want more.

We are the champions and our boys play like champions even though there's nothing to play for at all. Marcin Wasilewski slots in at the back like he's been there all season. Jamie Vardy returns after his ban to stretch the Everton defence to breaking point. Andy King is everywhere. Poor, beleaguered Everton with their fans turning against manager Roberto Martinez and their team going through the motions – they don't stand a chance.

Six minutes in, Vardy nudges the ball past Everton goalkeeper Joel Robles to open the scoring after a pinpoint cross from King. The drizzle becomes a downpour halfway through the first half and there are waves of attacks from the team in blue.

A second goal is inevitable. This time it's Riyad Mahrez wriggling his way into the penalty area and King side-footing into the net when the ball breaks free on the edge of the box. King's goal is reminiscent of those he scored regularly in the Championship and League One. He's the perfect goalscorer on the perfect day. We're delirious.

Everton, on the other hand, look like they'd rather be at home. Plenty of their fans are still on Merseyside having sold their tickets to City supporters desperate to be here. There's a bit of trouble in the away end – someone's overstepped the mark and overstayed their welcome.

Half time brings an opportunity for the fans to take a breather. In contrast, the players look fresh despite coming towards the end of a ferocious Premier League season and the pace continues into an impressive second half showing. There are two City penalties: Vardy smashes one into the net and the other high into the crowd to remain one goal behind Tottenham's Harry Kane in the race for the Golden Boot. Leonardo Ulloa and Jeff Schlupp come on to pose the Everton defence further headaches. Demarai Gray is the final substitute in the closing minutes, affording Mahrez the most deserved of standing ovations.

Before Mahrez departs the pitch at King Power Stadium for what we hope is not the last time, Everton get a goal. Kanté even misses a tackle in the build-up, finally letting an opposition player past him after a season of stubbornness. Kevin Mirallas is the goalscorer, netting a consolation as he did at Goodison Park in the last game before Christmas.

This feels like the final game before Christmas too. Today's the day. The referee's whistle is met with approval. It takes an age for the podium to be set up. That's fine. We've waited 132 years. We can enjoy this sense of anticipation.

Alan Birchenall carries the trophy from the tunnel and places it in front of the podium.

The owners, Vichai and Aiyawatt Srivaddhanaprabha, emerge onto the pitch to warm applause.

Claudio Ranieri is next to appear: the manager of our lives, the man who made this possible and a man whose appointment drew apathy from many of us last summer. What a way to prove a point. For all those who doubted him, his gift was the Premier League trophy.

Ranieri's management team follow. We knew that retaining Nigel Pearson's assistants, Craig Shakespeare and Steve Walsh, was important for the club. We don't see the hard work that goes into making this dream reality but we appreciate it. They have each worked wonders to find the right players and help mould them into the perfect team.

Those players are introduced to the crowd one by one. We cheer them all. Kasper Schmeichel as his father watches on proudly; Ritchie De Laet, having won promotion to the Premier League earlier in the day with his loan club Middlesbrough; Danny Drinkwater, the conductor; Robert Huth, the man mountain; Jamie Vardy, the phenomenon. The list goes on and on. Heroes one and all.

Wes Morgan is the final player to be introduced. Steve Worthy, winner of the competition to find a City fan to present the trophy, prepares himself. We all prepare ourselves.

And then it's just you again. Surrounded by thousands but alone with your thoughts. You've never seen anything like this in your life. You may never see it again. Breathe. Concentrate. Most of all, enjoy it.

Morgan lifts his head back and closes his eyes as though the enormity of the occasion has finally sunk in.

You would do the same but you don't want to miss it.

Morgan holds the trophy with both hands. Ranieri clutches one handle. Together, as the rest of the players prepare to leap into the air and we prepare the most almighty roar, Wes Morgan and Claudio Ranieri lift the Premier League trophy above their heads and it's right there in front of you: something you never thought you'd see. Something nobody could have predicted. Something nobody thought possible.

You can't wake up.

This is real.

This is the greatest moment in the history of Leicester City Football Club.

Leicester City 3 (Vardy 2, King)

Everton 1 (Mirallas)

Team: Schmeichel, Simpson, Morgan, Wasilewski, Fuchs, Mahrez (Gray), King, Kanté, Albrighton (Schlupp), Okazaki (Ulloa), Vardy

THE SKIPPER

A ROAR WENT UP FROM THE AWAY END AT THE KING POWER STADIUM.

Thousands of Liverpool fans had a perfect view of Leicester City captain Wes Morgan with two hands on Reds striker Rickie Lambert. Dragging him down. Stopping him running. Getting sent off.

Morgan had already poked a weak clearance straight to Steven Gerrard and slumped to his knees after Gerrard's shot found the bottom corner of the net to put Liverpool 2-1 up.

It was December 2014 and Leicester City, it seemed, were going down.

We loved Wes but we had begun to doubt he had the quality to succeed in the Premier League. The sight of our confused captain helpless at another goal conceded had become all too regular.

Morgan's physical strength is almost unparalleled throughout English football, but there has been less prominence given to the mental strength he has required to consistently drive himself and his team-mates on to greater achievements. Any lingering doubts have been shrugged off over and over again like the attentions of a persistent opposition striker.

He was released by Notts County at the age of 15 and told he was overweight by coaches at his next club Nottingham Forest. Morgan responded by establishing himself as a leading Championship centre-back, playing over 400 times for Forest and being named in the divisional PFA team of the year in 2011.

Out of the blue came an opportunity to leave his beloved red shirt behind and head down the A46. Nigel Pearson, a man who knows a thing or two about leadership, was convinced Morgan could captain his team to the Premier League.

Some of us weren't so sure. We already had Sol Bamba, Matt Mills and Sean St Ledger. Did we really need another centre-back?

It didn't take long for any lingering doubts to disappear.

Morgan was named in the Championship's PFA team of the year for a second time in 2013. A setback at Vicarage Road. He pushed on.

He made the list again a year later, this time lifting the Championship trophy at the King Power. He pushed on.

He made the Football League team of the decade in 2015 but he wouldn't be leaving the Premier League any time soon: he had just led City to improbable survival despite an error-strewn beginning to life in the top flight.

And so to the penultimate game of this season and, remarkably, the statistic that sums up the greatest year of Wes Morgan's life. As the sun goes down on Saturday 7 May 2016, the number of times Morgan has made an error leading to a goal this season and the number of times he has lifted the Premier League trophy are exactly the same: once.

A roar goes up all around the King Power Stadium.

Thousands of Leicester City fans have a perfect view of Leicester City captain Wes Morgan with two hands on the Premier League trophy. Lifting it up. Holding it high. Becoming a legend.

38: CHELSEA (A)

Sunday 15 May 2016

COINCIDENCE AND CIRCUMSTANCE DICTATE A LOVE-IN AT Stamford Bridge on a gorgeous day in the capital.

We revelled in Chelsea's downfall in December: cheering their home defeat to Bournemouth as we made the long trip back from Swansea; ecstatic at beating the champions on our own turf nine days later; smug when that result led to the departure of José Mourinho.

Now we're revelling alongside them.

The pavements of the King's Road shimmer in the heat as a huge blue and white party takes over. Champagne corks pop high in the air and sail overhead before curving down towards the ground like a Marc Albrighton delivery.

As we make our way through the turnstiles, we are handed postcards congratulating us on our title triumph. These are the things that threaten to make it sink in – what our football club has achieved.

When the fixtures were released eleven months earlier, some of us thought we'd have to be four points clear of the relegation zone before the final day trip to the Bridge to ensure survival for a second successive season.

Instead, we're 46 points clear of the bottom three.

Thousands of blue flags swish from side to side in the away end, obscuring the guard of honour Chelsea's dethroned champions lay on for the new kings of England.

There are two changes to the team that demolished Everton: Jeff Schlupp and Shinji Okazaki are replaced by Demarai Gray and Danny Drinkwater.

The action on the pitch is a sideshow to what happens in the stands. We sing about being champions, about Claudio Ranieri, about Eden Hazard and Tottenham and the goal that brought thousands of people onto the streets of Leicester. The Chelsea fans join in with all of it – even standing to applaud when we sing about taking their trophy - and it's easy to forget there's a football match taking place. We are grateful we don't need a result and we can laugh at the score updates coming in from the north east where Tottenham are capitulating.

That game ends 5-1 to relegated Newcastle, meaning Tottenham finish below Arsenal. We also look like losing, to a second half Cesc Fàbregas penalty, until the ball falls to Danny Drinkwater on the edge of the box and he drills it past Thibaut Courtois into the bottom corner in front of a jubilant away end. It doesn't matter but we didn't want to lose.

Drinkwater celebrates with the entire team before making a point of heading to the fans. This season has been a collective effort.

We spill out onto the streets surrounding Stamford Bridge, clutching flags and banners and a lifesize cardboard cut out of Eden Hazard with a Leicester scarf wrapped around his neck.

This part of the country oozes money. The houses we walk past after the final game of the most magnificent season we've ever known are worth millions. It takes thirty seconds to pass property worth more than it cost to assemble our title-winning team. In the Premier League, money equals success. Chelsea fans expected to be hosting a party but nobody expected it to turn out like this.

As we wander through the streets of west London, we shield our mobile phone screens from the light and try to make sense of the league table.

Tottenham's defeat at Newcastle means Leicester City end up winning the league by ten points.

Ten points.

It turns out we had enough points to win the league after the trip to Sunderland in early April – even before the dark moment that came when Jamie Vardy was sent off against West Ham. Before the tension that preceded victory over Swansea. Before the visit to Old Trafford.

And after this, nothing will ever be the same again.

Chelsea 1 (Fabregas)
Leicester City 1 (Drinkwater)
Team: Schmeichel, Simpson, Morgan, Wasilewski, Fuchs, Mahrez (Albrighton), Drinkwater, King (Okazaki), Kanté, Gray (Schlupp), Vardy

THE MAESTRO

I TELL TO THEM DILLY DING DILLY DONG WHEN THEY ARE sleeping.

The statement that launched a movement – Dilly ding, dilly dong was Claudio Ranieri's impression of a bell, used in team talks when players aren't paying attention. It became the triumphant refrain of Leicester City fans heading for the Champions League.

Hey man, we are in Champions League. We are in Champions League, man! Dilly ding, dilly dong! Come on! Now we go straight away… to try to win… the title. Yes! Yes, man!

Throughout the season, members of the press appeared to grow frustrated at Claudio Ranieri's refusal to admit Leicester City were in a title race. Before his team reached 40 points, that was the only target. When that was close to being achieved, he set another one: 79 points. It seemed fantastical at the time even after a great first half of the season.

Then he talked about Europe. Then the Champions League. And when journalists wanted to talk about Jamie Vardy's suspension ahead of a crucial game against Swansea, Ranieri turned the tables. He congratulated his players on qualifying for the Champions League and finally, four games from the end of the season, admitted his players were trying to achieve the impossible. That they did owed more than a little to Ranieri's mastery of psychology.

When we make a clean sheet, I pay to everybody a pizza.

Ranieri's used the media to convey several messages to players and supporters throughout the season. The promise of pizza for a clean sheet was not just a sound-bite. It was designed to show just how important the defensive side of the game was to him. He also made reference on more than one occasion to his desire to introduce Italian tactics to augment City's passionate approach.

When the clean sheets started to arrive, pizza ovens in the Italian restaurants of Leicester went into overdrive. Fans saw the two go hand in hand. Clean sheet. Pizza. Clean sheet. Pizza. By the end of the season, as Ranieri's troops delivered clean sheets week after week, even the most ardent pizza lovers were starting to get sick of the taste. By then, we had long since fallen for Claudio.

I say my team is like the RAF. It's fantastic. I love it.

Leicester City's magnificent defensive record in the second half of the season caused many to forget the wonderful forward play that characterised the beginning of the campaign. The pace and direct approach of Jamie Vardy, Riyad Mahrez and Jeff Schlupp terrified every defence City faced.

Ranieri was yet to strike the perfect balance that brought the title but he still publicly recognised the quality of his attacking talents.

Jamie Vardy, for example. This is not a footballer. This is a fantastic horse. He has a need to be free out there on the pitch.

Riyad is our light. When he switches on, wow! Leicester change colour!

At the forefront of City's attacking threat throughout the season, Vardy and Mahrez have had to cope with a stratospheric rise in interest from all quarters – football fans all over the world, the international media and, of course, opposition defenders.

Instead of playing down their importance to the team, Ranieri sought to give them confidence by underlining their need to produce. We knew Vardy would work hard without the ball and Mahrez was capable of magic when possession was won but Ranieri trusted them in all facets of the game. He backed Vardy as a central striker leading the line as the focal point of the attack and believed in Mahrez's ability to carry out his defensive duties.

Of course, they needed some help.

This player Kanté, he was running so hard that I thought he must have a pack full of batteries hidden in his shorts. He never stopped running in training.

I had to tell him, 'Hey, N'Golo, slow down. Slow down. Don't run after the ball every time, okay?'

He says to me, 'Yes, boss. Yes. Okay.'

Ten seconds later, I look over and he's running again.

I tell him, 'One day, I'm going to see you cross the ball, and then finish the cross with a header yourself.'

One of Ranieri's biggest masterstrokes was trusting N'Golo Kanté and Danny Drinkwater to play as a central midfield pairing. Gökhan Inler, City's marquee summer signing, was quickly sidelined as Ranieri realised he had two players with the drive and ability to dominate three-man midfields despite the numerical disadvantage. The wingers tucked in and Shinji Okazaki dropped deep to help out, but Kanté made it all possible.

Yes, big revenge! I want to kill him!

Ranieri's light-hearted response to a question about whether a forthcoming home game against Watford in November would provide an opportunity for revenge over their manager Quique Sánchez Flores, who had replaced him at Valencia a decade earlier, was perfectly pitched.

It was clear Ranieri thought the question was silly. Who knows how Nigel Pearson would have responded? We were split over Pearson's increasingly hostile press conferences during the course of the 2014/15 season, but opinion on Ranieri quickly became universal. We loved him. And we told him so whenever we could.

The Leicester fans I meet in the street tell me they are dreaming. But I say to them, 'Okay, you dream for us. We do not dream. We simply work hard.'

Ranieri's mantra throughout the season – the fans can dream, the players cannot – brought to mind the tifo display ahead of the opening game against Sunderland: 'Your colours are in our hands, our dreams are in yours.'

Together, we can achieve great things.

With a little help from a maestro.

38 AND A BIT: THE VICTORY PARADE (H)

Monday 16 May 2016

THE CITY IS AN EXPLOSION OF COLOUR AND NOISE.

Monday 16 May 2016: a day Leicester will never forget. People talk about cities having atmospheres at pivotal moments in history, about the streets crackling with excitement or anticipation or tension. Is it possible? Atmosphere enveloping an entire city? Affecting hundreds of thousands of people?

We know it is possible because we have lived it.

Hundreds of thousands of people descend on the city of Leicester for a victory parade worthy of the most unbelievable champions in the history of English football.

This is also a day that will help transform Leicester: the place, not just Leicester: the football club. As the title came closer, the international media descended on the city to tell the story of how the club's success has affected people's lives. Many have opened their articles or television reports by referring to Leicester as unremark-able. It may benefit the global audience to place the city in context but the tag is disparaging.

Leicester is a remarkable city: innovative, historic, multicultural – the birthplace of DNA fingerprinting, the resting place of King Richard III and a place where around 70 different languages or dialects are spoken.

Spending the day in this beautiful city bathed in sunshine is reminiscent of the opening day of the season when fans sat on pavements outside pubs and wondered what lay ahead. We could never have known it would eventually lead to this.

We gather along the route: a gigantic, swirling mass of people. In the city centre, all doors are open. We move in and out of pubs and shops and restaurants as though the whole city has been made available to us. We hear of others packed onto the platforms of nearby railway stations waiting to join the biggest party Leicester has ever seen.

There are people of all ages; some too young to fully comprehend what they are experiencing, some old enough to remember when the city's football team set off for London three times in the 1960s but returned without the FA Cup to parade for its people.

Now the open-top buses nudge along the High Street with the Premier League trophy front and centre. Claudio Ranieri stands behind it like a proud father, surrounded by the players he has described as being like his sons.

Blue and white tickertape rains down. The Clock Tower, a meeting point for decades, rises out of a sea of people like a lighthouse.

New Walk, a pedestrian path leading south from the city centre, plays host to a jubilant procession of those wanting to join the party that started early in the afternoon at Victoria Park, where the players and management will take to the stage at the end of the parade.

It takes over an hour for the buses to reach their destination. Along the way, they pass people hanging out of windows, standing on top of telephone boxes, on top of buildings. Some sit triumphantly atop traffic lights that change pointlessly from red to green and back again as thousands stand in the roads below. Their arms are spread wide and they lead the songs.

Victoria Park looks like a blue Glastonbury. People as far as the eye can see. We try to capture the moment on camera phones but the results don't do it justice.

Eventually, the players are introduced onto the stage one by one. A huge roar greets N'Golo Kanté, the shy Frenchman who came to help revolutionise our team and the most-coveted of our players. We hope it will make him stay.

As the sun goes down on Victoria Park, Leicester rock band Kasabian take to the stage. Frontman Tom Meighan, a City fan, introduces their first song with the words: 'This is for the underdogs.'

They tear through four songs, closing with 'Fire'. Each chorus, the same blast we hear vaguely above the din whenever City score a goal at home, is greeted with similar scenes to those in the stands after the ball hits the net.

Fireworks rise high above the terraced houses surrounding Victoria Park, fizzing and crackling in the fading light. The last clouds of smoke evaporate and we start to make our way home, shattered and glorious.

THE MESSIAH

WE NEVER THOUGHT WE WOULD SEE OUR TEAM WIN THE
Premier League. We never thought we could ever become champions of England.
We would have settled for a repeat of the late 1990s when another charismatic
manager recruited and motivated a set of misfits and rejects and turned them into
Leicester City legends.

Martin O'Neill managed City for less than five years but his achievements were
spectacular: promotion within months of being appointed, four consecutive top-ten
finishes in the Premier League, two League Cup wins and another appearance in the
final. He was our messiah.

O'Neill's aim in his first season managing in the top flight was survival. By April,
City had qualified for Europe for the first time since 1961.

'When we went up, we knew we would find the first quarter of the season very
difficult because we needed a little bit of time for players like Neil Lennon, Muzzy
Izzet and a young Emile Heskey to get acclimatised to the faster pace of the Premier
League,' says O'Neill.

'Some of the other players had experience of the league but essentially we knew we had to fight through that early period as a team. Eventually we finished in the top ten and won the League Cup, so we had immediate European football. I think our ambition then was starting to grow.'

This was a fantastic time to be a Leicester City fan. We had gone from the brink of the old Third Division at the beginning of the decade to seeing our team compete with, and often beat, some of the Premier League's greatest ever players and managers. We enjoyed four years of glory and eagerly waited for our club to take the next step. O'Neill had grand plans.

'In 2000, we had won the League Cup for the second time and the team was definitely taking proper shape,' he says. 'We were disappointed Emile Heskey had gone to Liverpool but we were going to use some of that £11million – a lot of money in those days – to try and strengthen the team.

'Ambitions for European football through the league were definitely growing.'

As we planned for our second European trip in four years, the news every Leicester City supporter had been dreading arrived. We had managed to help prevent O'Neill's departure when Leeds United came calling in 1998 but the lure of a challenge north of the border two years later proved too great for him to resist. He was leaving, 'called away to Celtic' as he puts it.

O'Neill became Celtic's most successful manager since the legendary Jock Stein during five trophy-laden years. When he returned to England in 2006, his aim was Champions League football with Aston Villa.

Did winning the Premier League ever feel like a possibility with Villa?

'No,' says O'Neill. 'But we finished in the top six for three consecutive years. And the final year was our best in terms of points total, so we were improving all the time.

'In our penultimate league game of that final season we went to Manchester City still harbouring ambitions of being in the top four. So I think Villa is unfortunately somewhat of a mess now but at that time it looked as if we could achieve our aim of Champions League football.'

Six years on, Champions League football is what we can look forward to at Leicester City and O'Neill is thrilled for the supporters, who he feels have contributed to the club's success.

'It's very important for players to create a bond with supporters,' he says. 'People should never underestimate the power of the supporter. Certainly with Ireland they have helped us enormously in our qualification for the Euros, and it was the same at Filbert Street.'

Comparisons have been made between this City side and the team O'Neill built but the man himself agrees with Emile Heskey that collective effort has been the most important factor.

'I could draw many parallels between individuals – too numerous to mention – but I feel that both sides had this great camaraderie and team spirit that was very evident in their play.

'Leicester have had the season of a lifetime. It's the first time they've won the league in their history and that is an enormous achievement by any standards, let alone in the current climate of Premier League football.'

For Leicester City to even be in the Premier League by 2016 felt the most distant of dreams for years after the club Martin O'Neill left in rude health was ruined by the mismanagement of others. It felt distant when we were demoted to the third tier for the first time in 2008. It felt distant when we suffered play-off heartache at Vicarage Road in 2012. It even felt distant in March 2015 when a 4-3 defeat to Tottenham Hotspur made relegation seem inevitable.

But you've got to be in it to win it.

Somehow, we were.

Somehow, we did.

THE UNBELIEVABLES

IN YEARS TO COME, WHEN OLD MEN AND WOMEN TELL THEIR grandchildren about the year they saw Leicester City win the Premier League to become champions of England, the stress and tension of March and April may be forgotten. The final league table, showing City ten points clear of the nearest challengers, does not convey the nervousness of those weeks as Tottenham Hotspur kept up the pressure.

Sunday 24 April 2016 saw the disappearance of the last nerves on display in the stands. It took another eight days for the title to be confirmed but that sunny afternoon it began to feel like a matter of time rather than a dream hanging in the balance.

In the closing moments of the game against Swansea, a cry went up from the Kop.

4-0 to the one-man team!

We tried to sing along through the laughter. It encapsulated everything.

It encapsulated the importance of individuals.

We were singing about Jamie Vardy, whose rise has rewritten the hopes, aspirations and possibilities of every footballer in the world, watching that day from an executive box as his team-mates rose to the challenge of coping without him.

We could have been singing about Riyad Mahrez, the PFA Footballer of the Year, or N'Golo Kanté, the Leicester City Players' Player of the Year.

It encapsulated the pre-eminence of the team.

Without Vardy, our team was still capable of magnificent performances. With him, the team remained more important than any individual – something re-iterated in numerous interviews by both Vardy and Mahrez as they coped admirably in the unprecedented spotlight.

Claudio Ranieri and his coaching staff had taken this team and constructed a machine – when we didn't have the ball, our eleven men moved up and across the pitch like table football players held in place by metal bars while Ranieri gestured from the touchline to keep the shape and stay compact.

When the ball was won, invariably by the peerless Kanté, the RAF would take over, our lightning attackers bearing down on goal from all angles.

It encapsulated the celebration of an incredible season.

The Swansea game felt defining both in the build-up and the aftermath, but there were so many defining moments before that day.

Incredible comebacks against Aston Villa, Stoke and Southampton in autumn placed a marker for what this team was about. Jamie Vardy's record-breaking goal against Manchester United in November was celebrated by players, officials and supporters as a collective achievement and recognised as such by Vardy himself. Three-goal romps at Newcastle and Swansea either side of Vardy's big moment showed our team could destroy inferior opponents with ease.

Then came the supposedly tough run of fixtures during which we would be found out. Or so they said.

It took moments of individual brilliance from Vardy and Mahrez to beat the champions, Chelsea, in the last home match before Christmas but they were highlights of another impressive team performance. Vardy didn't score again until the final game of January and Mahrez missed penalties against Bournemouth and Aston Villa that cost four points in total, yet sandwiched in between those games was a remarkable, backs-to-the-wall effort at White Hart Lane which saw Robert Huth's header secure three vital points against a title rival.

Some of us weren't sure at that point whether we were in a title race but the four games that followed the disappointing display at Villa Park made it crystal clear. Vardy returned to form with an excellent goal against Stoke and the goal of his life against Liverpool. Mahrez was also back to his best, producing a nutmeg of genius to fox Stoke's Philipp Wollscheid and the best long ball of the season to provide Vardy with an opportunity to crash the ball over Simon Mignolet.

All well and good but Manchester City would put us in our place. Or so they said.

An hour into the game at the Etihad, Leicester City published the following tweet:

So if you're just joining us.... #lcfc are leading 3-0 and Robert Huth is on a hat-trick! #MncLei

That captured the disbelief brilliantly in less than 100 characters, without even referencing another well-drilled defensive display and the Mahrez goal that stunned the world.

On Valentine's Day, the sight of Arsenal players celebrating on the pitch and in the changing room strengthened the resolve of our own team while the scenes outside the Emirates Stadium after the final whistle re-inforced the City fans' belief that this was our year, not theirs. Sing and dance all you want: our team won't wilt under the pressure.

We won five of the next six games, all by one goal to nil. That run looked like being extended until Jamie Vardy spoilt it all by netting a second at Sunderland. We can reflect upon that day now as the time we reached the points total needed to win the title.

Of course, we didn't know that then. We were worrying about West Ham and we feared it would all end in heartbreak when Jonathan Moss dismissed Vardy and points were dropped for the first time in six weeks.

So we were nervous ahead of the Swansea game.

Without Vardy, even another terrifyingly tight 1-0 win would do.

The result?

4-0 to the one-man team!

It encapsulated everything.

A glorious response from our players, heralded with humour by a set of supporters finally able to enjoy the greatest team we have ever seen.

Perhaps our achievement will never sink in.

After confirmation of Leicester City's status as 2016 Premier League winners and champions of England, players gave countless interviews about what they had accomplished.

To a man, they all summed it up with the same word:

Unbelievable.

Even they couldn't believe it.

These heroes. These history-makers. These legends.

The Unbelievables.

ACKNOWLEDGEMENTS

THANK YOU TO EVERYONE WHO HAS SUPPORTED, PRE-ORDERED or bought this book. It means everything.

Thanks Mum for making me interested in words and stuff. And reminding me to try to enjoy this...

Thanks Dad for taking me to Filbert Street. I was already thankful for that when we were in League One, never mind all this.

And Rhys, my brilliantly linguistic little brother: if Italy calls and want this book to be translated, I'm going to get you on the phone...

Thank you to Katy – what a season. Here's to that balloon at Bournemouth, being stuck in Stoke and just being there for all of it. And you can finally sing about winning the league, you superstitious sod...

Thank you also to Ella, Ann, Nat, Graeme, Alan and the Aussie Foxes. We did it.

Thank you to Haydon and Jo and Matt and Ruth for understanding my Leicester City obsession and its detrimental effect on social occasions...

Thank you to Alex Marsh and his receding Champions League hair with his chicken tikka dripping all over Filbert Street.

Thank you to Union FS, particularly James and Jamie for the interviews (plus, by extension, Julian – Up the Freundschaft!) and, more importantly, to everyone in SK1, for helping to make the home atmosphere something special.

Thank you to Lisa and Carl, Gail and Jason and all the staff at The Font for the pre-match of champions. And to Meesh and Macca, especially for New Year! Got to be a tradition…

Thank you to the FT lot. I'm going to forget somebody here but: Finners, Justin, Craig, Monk, Tommeh, Ched, Bert, Maybes, Wils, Shaun, Jay, James, Bilo, Lib, Joe Dot, Ben, Sparky, Robbo, Svenska, Sharman, Roo, Raj, Smuts, Mablo, Tadders, Stan, Chloe, Roy, Holly, Woolers, Matt, Miquel, Una, Scouse, Babs, Davie and, of course, Mark.

Thank you to Richard, Emma, Tom and the rest of the team for the support – the next one will be about accessibility…

Thank you to Room 90 for listening to me bang on about Leicester City endlessly.

Thank you to Jo for the phone charger that allowed me to interview Emile Heskey!

Thank you to the interviewees: Ian Stringer, Michael Regan, Jon Holmes, Andrew Taylor, James Johnson, James Sharpe, Jason Becker (and Jordan), Glenn and Nic Bradbury, Chris, Ken, John Hutchinson, to Emile Heskey (and Dan at Bolton Wanderers) and to Martin O'Neill (and Ian Mallon and Gareth Maher at the FAI).

Thank you to the proof readers, fact checkers and feedbackers: Tom Taylor, you're a star, cheers - and McEvilly, you're a genius.

Thank you to Dave Williams for the brilliant cover illustrations.

Thank you to James Corbett and Simon Hughes at Decoubertin for taking a chance on this and all your support.

Thank you to Claudio and to Jamie Vardy, Riyad, N'Golo… I won't name you all but hopefully some of you will read this and enjoy it. We certainly enjoyed watching you this season.

Thank you to everyone who ever cared about Leicester City Football Club. We'll always have 2016!

Lastly, thank you to my Grandad, Bryn, who would have been 100 this year – I think you'd have enjoyed reading this. I'll end this how you ended my first autograph book in the early 1990s…

By hook or by crook, you'll be last in my book.

Your football pal,

David